TUNE GOD IN

Your Heart's His Receiver

By Donna VanHorn

Inspired insights for daily living as seen through the
eyes of a wife, mother and grandmother

xulon PRESS

DEDICATION

To God the Father, God the Son, and God the Holy Spirit, for inspiring me and strengthening me in this holy endeavor. This work is all His doing – to bring honor, praise and glory to His name.

ACKNOWLEDGEMENTS

———————— ❋ ————————

*T*o Jesus Christ, my Lord and Savior, for His love and saving grace that make it possible for me to be in this place, at this time, doing what I do for His praise and glory.

To my husband Jerry, for his encouragement and patience, as well as his journalism background that helped smooth over the rough edges of my raw prose.

To my daughters Michele and Sarah, for their love for me and for being my loudest cheerleaders – as well as the innocent source of many of the devotions printed here.

To my friends Mary, Lynn, and Kari, for being in my face regularly with high-volume excitement and encouragement for this project.

To my Snowflakes and Triple D Bible study group, for their faithfulness in meeting together in my home to bask in God's Word – and offering inspiration for some of the "a-ha moments" reflected in this book.

To my team at Xulon Press, for making the publishing process so comfortable and enjoyable.

To Celebrate Recovery, for helping restore my husband, and as a result my family, to wholeness in Christ.

To my son-in-law Brad for allowing me to use photos of the RCA console radio in tribute to its owners: his parents Paul and Norma.

INTRODUCTION

————————✳————————

$\mathscr{I}$t was 2002, and my good friend Kate asked me to join her in opening the coffee shop she'd dreamed about for years. I did – and the ChitNChat coffee shop became a daily haven of prayer for dozens of customers [see Today's Christian Woman, March/April 2004, "Would You Like Prayer With That Latte?"] I think that's when she and I decided we'd launch a Bible study in my living room for our close friends and workmates. I'd never given much thought to what it would be like to lead a group like this. From previous experiences over the years, I knew what I didn't like about other peoples' leadership styles. I tried to give each session to God as I prepared, and He came through.

Fast forward to 2012. My husband and I were having a difficult time because of some poor choices he'd made. I realized our marriage was about to go under unless I found a way to give total control over to God through prayer and Bible study. The Bible study part was becoming easier, because of what I was learning from my Snowflakes and my Triple D groups. You'll read about them in the devotions. The hard part was giving everything to God; I confess I've been a "control freak."

It was kind of a "chicken and egg" phenomenon. I'm not really sure what came first: my decision to give it all to God and then roll with the flow, or God telling me He would take it all from me if I would simply surrender everything to Him. Bottom line was that both scenarios interacted simultaneously to produce a healing power through His grace I would have never thought possible. As a result, God through His Son Jesus Christ gave us the miracle of a restored marriage. And I'm now committed to share my story with others in any way that will encourage them in their own unique circumstances.

God laid it on my heart that He'd give me one or more words or short phrases every day or so, as the focus of my spiritual revelations that later would find their way into print. He's been faithful to that promise. Some days I've had to really scurry to keep up with Him, but that's the fun part of all of this. If God lays something on your heart, people, go with it! He'll make it exciting, rewarding, and fulfilling!

WELCOME!

*F*or reasons best known to God, He's nudged me to spend a few minutes with you each day, through this collection of devotional thoughts. I recently printed a booklet of spiritual vignettes based on insights shared within my small Bible study group, and gave it to my friends for Christmas. The positive feedback was immediate, overwhelming – and humbling. I believe God thus validated my gift of visualization, drawing word pictures in simple terms, to share Jesus with family and friends. So here we are. Each page builds on a single word or short phrase, and concludes with a relevant Bible verse. You're encouraged to look up the Scripture reference in your own Bible, since there may be several more verses in the passage that strengthen the context for you. I've grouped them according to major themes. Today's word is "Welcome!" If you've not met Jesus before, let the following pages introduce Him and move you to welcome Him into your heart. If you've already committed your life to Him, I pray these thoughts will strengthen your daily walk in the Christian faith.

Revelation 3:20 "Here I am. I stand at the door and knock."

NATURE

WILLOW

*T*here's a large weeping willow just outside our bedroom window. It's big enough that it's in various stages of dying and regeneration. There's an old branch that looks to me like it's close to death, but our condo's groundskeepers haven't gotten around to removing it yet. On closer inspection, it's leaning against younger, healthier branches. Without them, I'm guessing a strong wind or heavy snow (it's winter here as I write this) would bring it down. If you've read enough of my musings in this collection, you know I take much of my inspiration from God's natural world. In our time of need, God surrounds us with friends to support us and encourage us. We need to acknowledge those times of need, set aside our pride and sense of self-reliance, and let those loving folks come along side to shore us up.

Ecclesiastes 4:9-12 "Two are better than one, because they have a good return for their labor: If either of them falls down, one can help the other up (v9-10)."

DRY AND HOLLOW

❋

*S*everal times a week we drive by a large woodlot dominated by a handful of stately oak trees. It's unique, given that we live in one of the nation's fastest growing counties, and relentless real estate development has hemmed in this miniature forest. Toward the end of our Midwest tornado season, a major storm ripped through overnight. As we drove by the woodlot the next day, we noticed three of the large oaks had been torn apart down their main trunks. A closer look revealed the inside of the trunks had long since dried out and were hollow. Over the years, insects and disease had taken their toll, fatally weakening what had looked on the outside to be strong, healthy trees. We're like those oaks. We need a seamless relationship with Jesus, and through Him a confident dependence on the Holy Spirit to strengthen us against life's tornados. Without Him, we risk rotting from the inside out, and succumbing to the first wind that comes our way.

Ezekiel 37 1-14. "I will put my Spirit in you, and you will live."(v.14)

SNOWFLAKES

—————— ❄ ——————

We first met at a women's program at our church. A random drawing put us all at the same table. Over several sessions, we bonded, shared deeply personal issues, introduced our husbands to the circle – and committed to stay connected in mutual support and encouragement. It might have been because of the weather at the moment – one of us suggested we call ourselves The Snowflakes. We've continued to meet, not often but always purposefully. When we do, we eat, laugh together, experience meltdowns together, share family issues, offer insights for strength and resolution – and praise God for His faithfulness. In retrospect our group's name was appropriate. No two snowflakes are identical. But when bundled together, they cover the landscape's grit and grime with a pure white blanket. So it is with us. Each of us is special and uniquely made, individual personalities knitted together in God's love and grand plan, to help each other endure life this side of Heaven.

Isaiah 55:9-11 "The rain and snow come down from the heavens and stay on the ground to water the earth...so it yields...bread for the eater."

HOLY COMPOST

$\mathcal{F}$or years I've nurtured the visual of burying "junk" at the base of Jesus' cross. I can't remember exactly when it first came to me, but I'm sure it was at a time when I was struggling with some heavy burden that was getting in the way of my relationship with Him. The burial process is simple: during your quiet time, in your mind's eye, dig a hole at the base of the cross. Collect the day's garbage (regrets, sinful behaviors, hurts) and dump it all in the hole. Cover it thoroughly, tamp it down, and commit never to dig it up again. The outcome is amazing. The garbage turns into holy compost, and the burial plot begins to bloom with the fruits of the spirit: love, joy, peace, patience, kindness, goodness, faithfulness and self-control. Here's a big part of the miracle: unless you consciously choose to dig the junk up again (I can't imagine why you'd want to!), it's gone forever – Jesus has taken it from you. Hard to believe? Try it!

Galatians 5:22 "But the fruit of the Spirit is love, joy, peace…"

WHITE CHRISTMAS

❋

$\mathcal{I}$t had been a brown December, a continuation of the dry late summer and autumn we were experiencing. On the rare occasion of a light rain, especially late at night, I could look out my patio door and see the toads on the concrete, soaking in the moisture after crawling out of their shallow, dry burrows. December 25 was fast approaching, and the weather trends seemed the same. Then the TV weather forecaster began talking about the "remote possibility" of an approaching snowstorm. I haven't the foggiest (no weather pun intended) understanding about El Nino/ La Nina. I'm told the two of them apparently bear the blame for the year's meteorological extremes. The morning before Christmas, the official forecast was still iffy: "There might be some snow tomorrow." There was hope— down deep, the child in all of us wants a white Christmas. Early Christmas Day, it started. Light, fluffy, gentle. No threat to travel, just clean white flakes that gradually blanketed the ground. Unlike the weatherman's uncertain predictions, God says we can take His promises to the bank.

Hebrews 11:1 "Faith is confidence in what we hope for and assurance about what we do not see".

LIFE CANVAS

---❋---

*M*y local mall has a new store. When I first stepped in, I realized how much its theme appealed to my homespun decorating concepts. The store features unique clothing and interior accents. What caught my eye was a horizontal barn-board plank, probably 12 feet long, high on the wall behind the service counter. On it were hung dozens of used brushes encrusted with dried paint. Beginning with light pastels at the left end, the color palette transitioned to darker shades toward the right. Wow, I thought, this is a tapestry of my own life: light-hearted, carefree in my youth; struggles and issues in later years. There are lots of different "artistic" images out there, depending on how the audience perceives the artist's creation. This one especially touched my heart, and I let my heart keep imagining. God gives us the palette of our humanity, and we let Him paint the picture as we add the colors. What does your canvas look like? Do you, like me, have a specific color that dominates? As in a wild side of a splash of red (Satan)?

Genesis 9:16 "Whenever the rainbow appears in the clouds, I will see it and remember the everlasting covenant between God and all living creatures of every kind on the earth."

WILLOW 2

*I*t's snowing very hard here today. The wind is strong, approaching blizzard conditions. Schools are closed, and lots of scheduled community activities are being cancelled because of the weather. I just glanced out at the willow tree outside our bedroom window. Some of the smaller, frailer branches are now on the ground. It could be they were already dead but didn't show evidence of it. Maybe they were just too weak to withstand the howling wind. But there are others, some of them appearing just as frail, that are holding fast – and supporting much larger branches that earlier in the winter I'd considered dead or dying. An awesome picture!

Ecclesiastes 4:9-12 "Two are better than one, because they have a good return for their labor: If either of them falls down, one can help the other up (v9-10)."

IS SPRING NEAR?

———————— ✳ ————————

*E*ver wish you had a camera already in place so you could record something hilarious for "AFV"? That was me a couple of days ago, before the four-day thaw we were having. As I watched, a robin (why hadn't he gone south with all the others?) was hopping along the walk near our patio. Stay with me now – this whole sequence happened in a fraction of an instant. He hit a small patch of ice. His legs skidded out from under him. He instinctively spread his wings to their full width to steady himself. The ice ended. His feet hit the dry pavement. He lurched forward onto his beak. He folded his wings, and looked around as if to see whether anyone had observed his embarrassment. After I finished laughing, I remembered the support God gives us with angels' wings when we slip and fall. Like the robin, we sometimes stumble on unanticipated circumstances and trip over unknown obstacles. He's there to put us back on our feet – if we'll trust Him to do so.

*Isaiah 40:31 "Those who hope in the L*ORD *will renew their strength. They will soar on wings like eagles; they will run and not grow weary, they will walk and not be faint."*

SPRING

*S*pring here in Iowa is a portrait of inconsistency. Regardless of what the calendar says, some years it's early, other times it seems like it's late. No matter. The weather is going to do what it's going to do. At this moment, it's still the first week of March, and temperatures – at least today – are in the low 70's. There might be a brief setback or two; I'm thinking there may still be a snow shower in the near future. But the crocuses (or is it croci?), daffodils and Easter lilies will stubbornly push their way up into the sun and mark the new season. And so will Easter itself. God sent His Son to this earth to teach us to love each other sacrificially. He also showed us what that sacrifice looks like by sending Jesus to the cross for our sins. And wonder of wonders, the Son rose from the grave to pave the way for our eternal life with Him. Spring: the loveliest of the four seasons.

John 3:16 "For God so loved the world that He gave His one and only Son, that whoever believes in Him shall not perish but have eternal life."

THE WINDOW

$\mathcal{I}$'m not sure why, but over the years I've developed a habit of walking to one of my windows with cordless phone in hand when a friend or relative calls. I can definitely zero in on the conversation, but there's a part of my brain that can also register what my eyes are seeing beyond the window glass. When it's my daughter Sarah on the line, she can tell just from the sound of my chatter that I'm staring out the window. Her constant chiding me about my habit ended abruptly a few days ago. She found herself at her own window while we were talking – and I heard her gasp. "What's wrong?" I asked. "Mom," she said, "I just saw a red-headed woodpecker. And two sparrows are fluttering at their reflections in the window as we're speaking!" God's creation is all around us. It just takes a little redirection in our focus to see it – and take it all in.

Job 12:7-10 "But ask the animals, and they will teach you, or the birds in the sky, and they will tell you (v7)."

THE WOODPECKER

*M*igraine headaches are a curse I've endured for years. Thankfully, in recent times, I've found safe medications that help me manage the worst of the pain. I've also found solace in surrendering most of the source of those migraines – stress – to God in prayer. Watching a downy woodpecker yesterday was a great reminder of how the Lord and I together have managed those migraines. Have you ever watched a woodpecker work his way up a dying tree trunk? Once he's found a soft spot in the bark where tasty insects are likely hiding, he begins a rapid-fire drilling with his beak to uncover his next meal. If that won't cause a headache, nothing will. Sound like beating your head against a wall out of frustration? It reminds me of one definition of insanity: doing the same thing over and over, expecting a different result. How about this? Just take it to God in prayer, and trust He'll answer with the right solution.

Psalm 103:2-3 "Bless the Lord, o my soul, and forget not all His benefits, who forgives all your iniquity, who heals all your diseases."

SPRING RAIN

---※---

*S*ometimes rain is associated with personal trouble, as in "into every life a little rain must fall." But no matter where you live, the spring rains also bring the promise of new life. As I write this, it's almost the start of Holy Week, beginning with Palm Sunday and ending with Easter Sunday. Let's see if I can draw some parallels here. Each of us at some point in our lives has experienced a "holy week," a time that begins with our hopes of something special about to happen. Suddenly, those hopes are dashed and we plunge into despair. Then, at the last minute, there's a reprieve that restores our hope and refreshes our confidence for the future. According to Scripture, Jesus was cheered as Israel's hope by the throngs who welcomed Him on Palm Sunday. By week's end, He was dead – only to rise again on the following Sunday to proclaim eternal life for all who believe. Kind of like the spring rain clouds that temporarily dampen the landscape before bringing green grass and awakening sleeping flowers.

John 11:25 "I am the resurrection and the life. The person who believes in me, even though he dies, will live."

FLOODS

*N*oah had advance warning. We didn't. It was spring, and we'd just moved from southeastern Wisconsin to northeastern Iowa and our new home in Waterloo. The house had a split foyer floorplan. Our master bedroom and two other rooms, along with the laundry/mechanical area, were in the lower level. One night as we slept, a rain storm blew up, drenching the neighborhood with an inch-per-hour downpour. When we awoke, we stepped out of bed into a half-foot of cold water. The sump pump in the laundry room had failed to keep up with the volume of rainwater seeping down along the foundation. Not only did it ruin our bedroom furniture and new carpeting, all of our still-unpacked storage cartons were floating in another room. Maybe that's why the town was called Waterloo. What a helpless feeling! In our panic, we saw only the damage, failing to remember God created water as a blessing. It reminds me that water is a powerful and positive symbol throughout the Bible, including the parting of the Red Sea and Jesus' baptism by his cousin John.

Isaiah 44:3 "For I will pour water on the thirsty land, and streams on the dry ground; I will pour out my Spirit on your offspring, and my blessing on your descendants".

GOING BACKWARD?

---❋---

The more time I spend in God's Word, the more I encounter marvelous stories and events I've missed before, stories that testify to His power, might and faithfulness to His obedient followers. That list is endless, but the one I'm thinking about here is the day Joshua and the Israelites finally entered their Promised Land by crossing the Jordan River (see Joshua 3 and 4).The river was at flood stage, but when the priests carrying the Ark of the Covenant (symbolic of God's promises) stepped into the water, it began flowing backward upstream! It's happened in more modern times. For example, in 1812, severe earthquakes along the New Madrid Fault caused the Mississippi River to reverse course for several hours. Sometimes we experience life events that make us feel like we're uncontrollably rushing backwards. If we're in Christ, the truth is we're actually moving forward toward greater faithfulness and greater blessing. It just doesn't feel like it at the time. Trust Him. He'll keep the momentum going in the right direction.

Joshua 3:16: "The water from upstream stopped flowing. It piled up in a heap a great distance away."

CACTUS FLOWER

------------ ✳ ------------

I'm told there are more than 1,400 different species of cactus. For many of us the most familiar is the tall, multi-armed suguaro that's native to Arizona. But all species have two things in common: they produce beautiful flowers during the few weeks of their blooming season – and they have sharp needles. I've come to understand that God puts "cactus people" in my path on a regular basis. These are folks with a prickly personality attributable to any number of causes: insecurities, pain, abuse – the list is endless. At first glance, they're beautiful people. Their multi-color blossoms draw me to them before I feel the prickly spines. I'm guessing you wouldn't want to hug a cactus. Yet God calls me to care for them. I'm powerless to do that on my own. The only way it's possible is to let God's love flow through me, creating His holy armor for protection against the sharp spikes. Then I can focus on the blooms and ignore the "prickles".

Matthew 7:16 "By their fruit you will recognize them. Do people pick grapes from thorn bushes, or figs from thistles?"

MOURNING DOVE

---❋---

*T*his spring we have a pair of mourning doves – called turtle doves in some parts of the country — nesting in the rooftop rain gutter outside one of our windows. I've wondered why the gutter, where a heavy downpour could wipe out their homestead. Since they're part of God's creation, I trust their instincts. I knew they usually mate for life, but I was curious about their other habits. A quick check of websites revealed these interesting facts: the female picks the nesting site; although the male forages for building materials, it's the female who actually builds the nest; the male sits on the eggs during the height of the day, but she's the one who pulls the all-night incubation shift. And as part of the pigeon family, she feeds her babies "crop milk" – a regurgitated cottage cheese-like substance for their first few days. Just like a woman – taking charge when most needed. The only contradiction in this comparison? It's the male who does the most talking. Go figure!

Proverbs 31:10-31 "A wife of noble character who can find? She is worth far more than rubies…She watches over the affairs of her household and does not eat the bread of idleness…"

BIRD WATCHING

————————— ❋ —————————

*N*ormally I avoid using words with more than three syllables, but here goes: <u>ornithologist</u>. I guess you could call me an amateur…well, one of those people. As you've discovered in these pages, I enjoy absorbing nature, whether while traveling or simply looking through my patio door. This week it was the patio door that framed my nature walk. A robin and a red-winged blackbird were both foraging on the lawn. Having a basic knowledge of both species, I figured the robin was grubbing for worms and the blackbird was harvesting seeds. From the same source, both were finding nourishment for their bodies. Ready for this? We all go to God's Word, the Bible, for different reasons. Some of us seek reassurance in times of self-doubt, others seek wisdom and direction when facing indecision, and still others seek the peace that comes from merely resting in His loving arms. But no matter what the motivation, we all go to the same source for the same reason. We all need God-given nourishment – food for the soul.

John 6:35 "Then Jesus declared, "I am the bread of life. Whoever comes to me will never go hungry, and whoever believes in me will never be thirsty."

STRANGE LANGUAGES

---- ❋ ----

*T*he Grand Canyon is one of God's most awesome creations. Scientists attribute this geological marvel to the work of millions of years of earth crust shifts and the carving work of the Colorado River. Simply put, it was God who painted this beautiful landscape that we were privileged to visit recently. Although I'd been there as a teenager, it was my husband's first trip. Neither of us was disappointed. For me, I was struck as much by the myriad foreign languages of the other visitors rubbing shoulders with us, as I was with the natural beauty in front of us. At first, I was reminded of the Towel of Babel (Genesis 11), when God caused confusion among people's languages because of their idol-worship. And then I remembered Pentecost (Acts 2) when God's faithful gathered to worship – and in an act of restoration by the Holy Spirit, they were able to understand each other's foreign languages. Although I wasn't sure what some our fellow tourists were saying, it was very clear they were all remarking about the natural beauty that lay before us.

Acts 2:7-8 "Utterly amazed, they asked: 'Aren't all these who are speaking Galileans? Then how is it that each of us hears them in our native language?'˝

WORDS

IT'S HOW YOU SAY IT

------------- ✳ -------------

In case you missed the title of this book, flip back to the cover. Now pay attention, because what I'm about to tell you starts with tuning in your radio. It happened during one of my marriage's "life transitions." That's a ho-hum euphemism for "what the heck just happened and where are we going from here?" It was after my husband's unsuccessful foray into a political career (you'll read about that in a later devotion). He landed a job as news director and early morning news anchor at a suburban Milwaukee radio station. I used to joke that it was the only time in our life together that I could turn him off. The community's ethnic base was strongly German. Lots of folks there still spoke not only with remnants of the mother tongue accent, but also with a unique local dialect that was charming – and sometimes confusing. I was grocery shopping one day, and the cashier saw my name on my check. "Oh!" she exclaimed. "Are you Jerry VanHorn's wife?" I nodded yes, and then my jaw dropped when she added, "I woke up with your husband in bed this morning!" I knew she meant well, and I took her words as praise and encouragement. But it sure didn't come out that way.

Proverbs 12:25 "Anxiety weighs down the heart, but a kind word cheers it up."

SENIOR MOMENT

*O*ne never knows, but at this particular moment I'm thinking we've reached the bottom rung on the adult continuum of household downsizing. The reasons have always been logical, and for the most part the outcomes, in terms both financial and physical investment in upkeep, have proven worthy. Our two-bedroom first floor condo with a view of a pond and its yearly population of mallard families is cozy, attractive – and practical. The only exception to a workable floor plan is the narrow pathway through the dining area to the door to our attached garage. As we were leaving for errands yesterday, I was sitting on a dining table chair putting on my tennis shoes. My husband was trying to tie his shoes, too. He looked like a dog spinning around in a kennel, looking for a resting spot. "The only drawback to this place," he observed, "is this congestion here by the garage door while we're both getting ready at the same time." I agreed…and then added, "Yes, but five years ago, neither of us had to sit down to put our shoes on!"

Ecclesiastes 12:3 "Remember him before your legs – the guards of your house – start to tremble; and before your shoulders – the strong men – stoop."

ELOQUENT

I've never viewed myself as "eloquent." One definition of the word is "the ability to use language clearly and effectively." My kids snicker when they hear me utter mixed metaphors, such as "It's as hard as a brick-bath," or "You could have knocked me over with a fender." If I can't access Spellcheck on the spur of the moment, I'll usually turn to the person closest to me for help with spelling multi-syllable words. Yet, after I gave my Snowflakes group a little devotional book I'd written that captured some of their insights and inspirational comments, one of the members complimented me for being eloquent. While I feel honored and humbled by her praise, I still don't see myself in that particular light. I'd rather be remembered as a person who demonstrated her faith by her example and her love for others. If my friends see me as eloquent, I pray they appreciate that the real "eloquence" is actually God speaking through me.

James 2:18: "I will show you my faith by my actions."

MINISTRY

*W*ow. I'm thinking about how best to express this thought without it being "all about me." I guess I'll just let the words flow here, and pray God will help you see my heart in the right context. Ever since I first encountered the other women in our Snowflakes group, and grew together with them in studying the Word and enjoying their fellowship, I've been challenged to share Christ through the gifts He's given me. At the outset, I felt like Moses when he was first confronted by God. I knew what He was calling me to do, but I had no confidence in my ability to express myself outside my own family circle. Somehow the Holy Spirit drew me to Isaiah, one of God's most powerful and influential spokespersons. "He wakens me morning by morning, wakens my ear to listen like one being taught," the prophet wrote. Now here I am, leaning on Him and in some small way, leading others to Christ through small Bible study groups…and writing a devotional! What a rush.

Isaiah 50:4 "The Sovereign Lord has given me an instructed tongue, to know the word that sustains the weary."

THE CLARINET

I wish I could remember why I started playing the clarinet when I was in second grade. Maybe it was just because that's the instrument young girls learned to play when they wanted to be "in the band." In any event, Mrs. Pritchett became my private teacher and eventually my advocate. She leveraged me into the high school band while I was still in eighth grade. By the time I was a senior I was first chair. That year I was honored with the John Philip Sousa Award, and that year – what a hoot! — we represented our state in JFK's inaugural parade (OK, now you know how old I am). For two more years, I played in my college's concert band. And then it was over. I got married, got a job, and the clarinet collected dust. Until three decades later, when a friend mentioned her granddaughter wanted to start playing clarinet. I felt privileged to give my ebony Conn to her. I have no idea how that turned out. But I'm glad I could give it to someone who needed it. You can give Jesus as a Gift to someone in need. In fact, He calls you to do just that.

Psalm 96:2-4 "Tell everyone about the amazing things He does." (v3)

ANGER

$\mathscr{I}$'m no saint. Ask my immediate family, the people who know me best. On second thought, don't ask! I'm human. I get angry, just like you do. At the moment, I'm in a situation where I'm really upset with someone who's wronged me. Maybe upset is too mild an adjective. Hot, steamed, totally torqued – that kind of angry anger is like what I'm feeling right now. Funny thing is, I've discovered the longer I allow my anger to control me, I forget why I'm honked off. In times past, when I've been on the verge of being totally consumed with that kind of anger, I've found relief by taking my anger to God. Once I've confessed those sinful feelings, He's softened my heart and taken the anger from me. The sooner I do that, the better – or I risk adding fuel to the fire by barking back (Proverbs 15:1).

James 1:19-20 "Be slow to anger…for the anger of man does not produce the righteousness of God."

BODY LANGUAGE

---- ❋ ----

*S*ome people are non-verbal. Their primary mode of communication is by way of their body language: gestures, posture, facial expressions that let other folks know what they're thinking, how they're feeling. Still others are verbal. They choose to speak their mind and their heart, sometimes in gentle terms, often in not-so-gentle ways. No question about it, though. The verbal people get their message across, even if it cuts to the quick. Me? Long ago I figured out how to combine the verbal and non-verbal into one potent package! For me, the key is to punctuate what I say with an extended index finger. My husband says I need to get a license for a dangerous weapon. It's like I'm aiming a loaded pistol at the person to whom I'm directing my message. It gets their attention. It often gets laughs. But I've also learned it's hurtful, and I need to bring it under control. So I've started wrapping that finger in duct tape.

Proverbs 15:4 "A gentle tongue is a tree of life, but perverseness in it breaks the spirit."

EATING

---※---

My husband and I love to snack between meals. Sometimes it's nothing more than honey roasted peanuts or naked pita chips (my personal favorite). We also have a thing for sweet pepper relish, poured over cream cheese and spread on water crackers. There's a specific brand of relish we prefer; it's made by a food supplier in Massachusetts. You see, my husband's a native New Englander. To make matters better, even though retired, he works part time as a salad chef in the kitchen of a local supermarket, and comes home with all kinds of new snack items to try. At our age if we're not careful, we could find ourselves overeating. The words "gluttony" and "morbidly obese" come to mind. In the short run, the Word of God doesn't reward the human taste buds like honey roasted peanuts. In the bigger picture, though, it's what truly satisfies the soul – and according to Jesus' promises, leads us to eternal life with Him. Now <u>that's</u> a perfect snack!

Matthew 4:4 "But Jesus said, 'It is written, 'Man is not to live on bread only. Man is to live by every word that God speaks.'"

WRONG WORDS

───────── ❋ ─────────

*M*y husband and I share most of the household chores these days. He loves to cook; I love to let him. This morning I was busy with something else, so he offered to start a load of wash. "What temperature do you use to cook the bath towels?" he asked, and immediately knew he'd misspoken. We laughed together. Earlier in the morning, we had talked briefly about reconciling our checkbook together, a weekly task we refer to as "flossing." My husband suggested that tomorrow would be a good day to "flush the checkbook." Again, we chuckled at the slip, and the fact that it's happening with growing frequency as we age. The irony here is that he was an English major in college, and later an award-winning journalist. He's always prided himself on calling up the right word in the right context at the right time. At a deeper level, it's a reminder that we need to choose our words carefully. The wrong word spoken in a heated moment can cut to the quick.

James 3:1-12 "Consider what a great forest is set on fire by a small spark (v5b)."

AFFLICT THE COMFORTABLE

------------ ❄ ------------

*I*n one of his recent sermons, our senior pastor offered up one of the missions of Jesus Christ: "Comfort the afflicted…and afflict the comfortable." I'm one of those people who take folks at their word, and if I have to process something a little while…well, then I do the processing. This is one of those statements I needed to process. Here's what I came up with. For those who accept Jesus as their Lord and Savior, and who open up the gifts of peace and comfort He offers, even in times of great stress and trial, He will comfort them. It's a very simple promise. For those who think they've got it under control, that they can rely on their own resources to deliver them from trouble or conflict, God is going to find a chink in their armor to bring them to their knees and prompt them to confess their need for Him.

Psalm 18:27: "You save the humble but bring low those whose eyes are haughty."

DANCING

J enjoy spending time with my hair stylist, at least within the parameters of my regular appointments. Like all of us, she's still growing in her Christian faith. And she showers me with a barrage of faith-related questions whenever I'm there. On my last visit, she told me of an elderly man in her church, apparently someone relatively new to the congregation. During the worship songs, he could be seen dancing up a storm. The pastor asked him about it. The gentleman replied, "For nearly 80 years I was an atheist. Suddenly I got to know the real Jesus – and now I can't stop dancing!" We don't know what or who brought him to his decision for Christ. It might have been you. If it wasn't, you could be that someone for the next person in your life who's ready to hear the Gospel. Take the time to tell them. Crank it up!

John 9:1-30 "One thing I do know. I was blind but now I see! (v.25)"

"KISS" PRINCIPLE

———————— ❄ ————————

I don't give much thought to grocery shopping until it's time to finalize the list. In our house, that task is framed around our semi-monthly Social Security checks. And when we shop, it's pretty basic. Usually store labels, unless we know a brand name will better serve our needs and palates. So I was intrigued to browse through a new upscale "fresh market" grocery across the street from our usual store. "Wow!" I thought. "Look at all the choices – whoa, and look at the prices, too!" I subscribe to the KISS Principle: Keep It Simple, Sister. For me, that goes for not only my grocery shopping but also my relationship with Jesus. Way too many folks try to understand the how and why of who Jesus is before they'll give in to faith. It's simple. He is who He says He is: our Lord and Savior. He came to forgive our sins, and to give us an abundant life, if we'll simply trust His promises. Don't try to figure it out. Just believe.

1ˢᵗ Corinthians 2:5 "…so that your faith might not rest in the wisdom of men but in the power of God."

BUCKET LISTS

———————— ❈ ————————

*G*od has blessed us abundantly in many, many ways. One of them has been the gift of travel. No, we're not in the category of being able to take world cruises every month (I'm reminded of the ditzy lady who told an interviewer, "Last year I took a trip around the world. This year I'm going somewhere else!") But trips related to my husband's career have enabled us to enjoy Hawaii (the sunsets on Maui are gorgeous), the Pacific northwest, Florida's Gulf Coast, coastal road trips from Savannah to Maine…it's a really long list! My good friend Mary and I even spent 12 days together touring England and the Cotswolds. Lately Jerry and I have been picking away at our "bucket lists." Mine was to take all our grandkids on a roundtrip train ride to Chicago, including overnights at the Palmer House. Awesome! His was being at Talladega for a NASCAR event. Awesome – for him. At the very top of our remaining bucket lists: when we die, forever joining God in Heaven, where the New Jerusalem is made of gold and jewels (Revelation 21). I hope you'll join us there.

Luke 23:43: "Today you will be with me in Paradise."

TRADITIONS

---------------- ❋ ----------------

*M*y mother was heartbroken when, in 1964, the Milwaukee Braves announced the team would be moving to Atlanta for the start of the next season. From our home in southeastern Wisconsin, Mom loved listening to Braves broadcasts on the radio. I doubt she missed many, from the start of spring training through season's end. Although I was a teen at the time and focused on a love interest that would eventually turn into a lifetime marriage, I was bummed about the team's move too. After all, like everybody else in the known universe during the 1957 World Series, I was captivated by the play of Lew Burdette, Eddie Mathews, Hank Aaron (of course) – and my personal favorite, Andy Pafko. Fast forward. I'm sitting here watching the Cubs play the Royals in a spring training game televised from Mesa, AZ. The Cubs have been "my team" since I moved to Des Moines, where I've been able to watch prospective major league stars play for the Triple A Iowa Cubs. I love you, Mom. Apples don't fall far from the tree.

1 Corinthians 11:2 "Now I commend you because you remember me in everything and maintain the traditions even as I delivered them to you."

NO REGRETS PLEASE

---------------❋---------------

*O*ne of our state's wealthiest and most successful entrepreneurs died last week at the age of 79. I've become
captivated by his story, first as I read his obituary that failed
to mention any survivors but did include a detailed list of
beneficiaries of his philanthropy – a list that went on for
several paragraphs. A couple of days later I saw a news-
paper account that shed more light on what must have
been a lonely life. He gave away much of his money to
an endless list of worthy causes and institutions, and his
name graces the façade of hospitals and university build-
ings across the Midwest. The only child of his parents, he
himself was childless. As he told a reporter, "I couldn't
give enough of myself to hold together three different marriages." My mind jumps to Jesus. What if He had said, "I'm
too busy to go to the cross for you"?

*Ecclesiastes 4:4-12 "'For whom am I toiling,' he asked, 'and why
am I depriving myself of enjoyment?' (v8b)"*

INSTINCTS

*P*opeye was a man who learned to trust his instincts. I'm not talking about the spinach-eating cartoon character. This Popeye was better known as Don Zimmer, long-time MLB player, coach and manager, who died in 2014 at age 83. My Chicago Cubs were among the teams he managed. Zim is quoted as saying, "If you think of it, do it." From his sixty-year cache of baseball experience, he'd learned to let his instincts guide him in setting up on-field plays in critical situations. And baseball historians are already describing him as someone whose instincts were usually on target. Almost daily I think of someone in need of encouragement, or a situation needing my intervention. And then invariably my human tendency to second-guess myself kicks in. My husband's constantly in my face encouraging me not to retreat and reminding me these promptings to serve others are most likely from the Holy Spirit calling me to follow through. He's not alone with his counsel. A host of Bible scholars agree that when we're tuned in to God and His will for us, the Holy Spirit will lead us to act on Jesus' behalf. Trust those instincts!

John 16:13 "But when he, the Spirit of truth, comes, he will guide you into all the truth."

PATIENCE

FORGIVENESS

❊

*A*s I write this, I can hear the TV in the next room. Over live video from the scene, reporters are describing another tragic multiple-fatality shooting. Still unsure, they're reporting, whether it was the act of a deranged person or an organized terrorist assault. The distinction is irrelevant; I'm feeling "righteous anger" swelling in my gut. Whoever did this, make them pay big time, my head is saying. Our court system notwithstanding, my heart is simultaneously remembering that justice and revenge are ultimately our God's domain. Even closer to home, my Lord is pleading with me to have a forgiving heart. He doesn't excuse abusive or violent behavior. By His example, he condemns the act but has compassion on the actor. And He challenges me to do the same. It's not been easy. Some of those closest to me have hurt me over the years. Christ has shown me that holding grudges makes me the real prisoner. He alone gives me the power to forgive and move forward.

Luke 23:34 "Father, forgive them, for they don't know what they are doing."

JEALOUSY vs. CONTENTMENT

---***---

*B*eware of jealousy. It can creep up on you and over-take you before you know it's starting to consume you. Listen to me – when I say it can "consume you", I'm not kidding. Jealousy can devour you like a man-eating python, swallowing you slowly and relentlessly, until you suddenly realize it's too late for rescue. My life experiences define jealousy for me: wanting what someone else has. Having faced financial sacrifices in my life because of events beyond my control, I confess I've harbored envy toward friends. Not because of who they are, but because of what they have, compared to what I have…or don't have. Shrugging off that pervasive envy isn't easy, because we live in a material world that measures personal value in terms of possessions and wealth. But God, through His Word, and the contentment that flows to us through the Holy Spirit, can give us peace and confidence with who we are and what we have. He offers that contentment in the gift of His Son Jesus, but for us to bask in it, we need to claim it. Do it prayerfully, right now.

Philippians 4:11-13 "I have learned to be content no matter what the circumstances." (v.11b)

SALVATION

━━━━━━ ✳ ━━━━━━

I'm no theologian, but here's what I believe about death-bed conversions: they are just as valid in God's eyes as they are when a teenager accepts Jesus and experiences a life-long walk with Him. My husband's supermarket kitchen offers holiday meal packages from Thanksgiving through Christmas. Some people wait until the very last minute to place their orders, but the store promises them the same meal, same quality, same price, as those who ordered three weeks in advance. I love Jesus' parable of the vineyard workers. The ones who clocked in at the start of the shift grumbled when they got paid the same wage as those who clocked in later. Here's the good news: no matter when you surrender to Jesus, He'll accept you and make good on His promise that you'll someday be with Him in Paradise. The downside: unlike the shoppers, if you wait until the last minute, think of all those years of peace, contentment, and blessings you missed.

Matt. 20:1-16 "I want to give the one who was hired last the same as I gave you. (v14b)"

NEW YEAR

*M*y husband and I are die-hard Chicago Cubs fans. We try to make the six-hour trip from our house to Wrigley Field at least once a season, although budgets and other commitments sometimes get in the way. Otherwise, we're enjoying each game via TV or radio. Radio's our favorite, primarily because play-by-play announcer Pat Hughes is so good at what he does. Each broadcast begins with a montage of Cubs-related soundtracks, including a recording of the late Cubs third baseman Ron Santo yelling, "This could be the year!" It's New Year's Day as I write this. I'm wondering if this will be the year of our Lord's return. After all, the Bible promises that He will come on earth a second time *(Rev.22:12)*. But the Scriptures also say no one knows when that will happen *(Mark 13:32-33)*. Are you ready? If not, He wants you to come to Him, confess your dependence on Him, and let Him create a new heart for you. This could be the year!

2 Corinthians 5:17: "Therefore, if anyone is in Christ, he is a new creation; the old has gone, the new has come!"

FAITH NOT SIGHT

———— ✳ ————

$\mathcal{M}$y daughter's friend is a vivacious and successful entrepreneur. She's also a powerful example of how an intimate walk with Jesus can carry you through life's trials and tragedies. When her first husband walked out on her, leaving her to support and raise four young children, she remained steadfast in her faith. Her prayers for a more fulfilling and permanent marriage were answered in the form of a man of similar faith. Then tragedy struck again. Her new husband was diagnosed with a malignant tumor behind his eye. Surgery and follow-up treatment seem to have been successful, at least to date. We were together at a recent social event and I marveled at the naturalness of his prosthetic eye. I learned they've embraced his new "look" as a Christian witness that faith trumps frailties. Like me, she writes words of encouragement to others who are struggling. The letterhead of her customized notecards reads "We live by faith and not by sight."

2nd Corinthians 5:7 "We live by faith, not by sight."

ALL IN

$\mathcal{I}$n one of his professional roles my husband was a management consultant, providing his clients with leadership coaching designed to boost their companies' success. When it came to performance evaluations, he bristled at the term "weaknesses." He much preferred to call them "improvement opportunities." Okay, I get that. One of my own improvement opportunities is to back off on my judgmental tendencies. I look around at my friends and acquaintances who profess to believe in God because "they go to church." Wearing my judge's robes, when I hear that I think, at best, they're telling me they know who God is – but I'm also thinking they don't really know God. I cry silently for these folks. I want them to be all in, so they can know the fullness of His grace and the blessing of eternal life with Him. My God tells me He much prefers people to be <u>hot</u> for Him, not just lukewarm. Check it out at Revelation 3:16.

1ˢᵗ John 2:6 "Whoever claims to live in Him must walk as Jesus did."

PATIENCE

————————— ❋ —————————

*P*atience has never been one of my strong suits. Talk to any one of my family members, or friends from over the years. With a little prodding and a guarantee I'll not track them down, they'll tell you they've rarely seen me display patience. I'm okay with that. My philosophy says if it's worth doing, it's worth doing RIGHT THIS INSTANT! Depending on what it is, and where it is, and who it involves, the reality is it probably can wait. I need to work on cultivating a deeper and wider cache of patience. I know that. Thing is, I've also been told the more I pray for patience, the more stuff I'll encounter that will try my patience. Oh well, let's give it a shot. Come on, God! What are You waiting for?

Proverbs 14:29 "Whoever is patient has great understanding, but one who is quick-tempered displays folly."

SAVINGS ACCOUNT

———————— ❋ ————————

*W*hat I'm about to share may not resonate well with those of you who've been wise investors and prudent financial managers from the get-go. We've not been that astute. That is, until we became "seasoned citizens." As the German saying goes, "Too soon oldt, too late schmart." After working our way through a season of handling the final affairs of my husband's late mother, we realized the need for long term care insurance (something she did not have). We have what advisors would describe as a modest plan for ourselves, but at least it's in place to protect our kids from the burden of paying our nursing home bills if and when it comes to that. In order to cover the premiums, we've disciplined ourselves to make deposits to an accrual account from my husband's part-time retirement job. God wants us to be with Him in His kingdom for eternity, and He's willing to wait patiently for all those who are figuring out His spiritual accounting system.

2 Peter 3:9 "The Lord isn't slow to keep his promise, as some think of slowness, but he is patient toward you, not wanting anyone to perish but all to change their hearts and lives".

TEXT CHECK

———————— ✳ ————————

*O*ne of my favorite TV shows recently honored a 15-year-old for her invention of a smart-phone app that forces the user to reconsider a text message before hitting the "send" button. The audience applauded the concept, recognizing that it can prevent misunderstandings or even worse, broken relationships. God did that for me just the other day. I was thinking about e-mailing a close friend about a prayer concern. I knew the topic was potentially touchy, and so I talked with God about what to say and how to say it. Then I sat down at my laptop, opened up my Gmail account – and my mind went completely blank! I couldn't even remember what the prayer issue was, let alone who I was planning to e-mail and what I was supposed to say. God definitely answered my prayer for His guidance in the matter. In essence, He said, "Don't send it." Imagine how many hurt feelings could be avoided if each of us tapped God's "text check" before we spoke.

Proverbs 29:20 "Do you see someone who speaks in haste? There is more hope for a fool than for them."

UNFINISHED PAINTING

———————— ❋ ————————

*T*n his early 'teens, my husband was asked to serve as a model for a professional artist's portrait class. Every week Jerry would sit for two hours, as motionless as possible, while the artist's adult students sketched and painted. The artist would occasionally work at his own easel, demonstrating brush techniques and color combinations for his students. When the class ended, the artist gave Jerry the canvas he'd used as a teaching tool. But the portrait was unfinished, since it was merely the product of periodic demonstrations. After we married, that framed portrait hung in our home for years. It eventually became a metaphor for who we are while living out our earthly existence. Hopefully, each of us has accepted Jesus as our Leader and Forgiver, and experiencing the resulting joy. But until we finally are with Him in Heaven, joining God His Father and endlessly singing their praise, our portrait is unfinished.

Philippians 1:6"…he who began a good work in you will carry it on to completion until the day of Christ Jesus."

DID YOU HEAR ME?

———————— ❊ ————————

*I*t all started with a tiny four-ounce can of mushroom stems and pieces. My husband was making out his grocery list for a gourmet meal he was planning for us, and his recipe called for the mushrooms. I suggested he check our pantry first before heading to the store because I knew we had the can of mushrooms there. When he came back with the groceries, the bag included a can of mushrooms. As you read this, you're saying pretty much the same thing I said to him: "Didn't you hear me?" What do you do when it's obvious a child or spouse hasn't listened to you? First, decide whether it's a battle worth fighting. Then, be open to reviewing all the facts. In this case, my husband said he heard my suggestion, but in his hurry simply forgot to follow through. Conclusion: battle not worth fighting. It was just a tiny four-ounce can of mushroom stems and pieces.

James 1:19 "Everyone should be quick to listen, slow to speak and slow to become angry."

CHOOSE CAREFULLY

————————— ❈ —————————

A career advisor I was watching on TV was offering up her "Top Ten Tips for Success." Here's Number 4: "Don't Follow A Parked Car." My first reaction was to snicker. I pictured the unpleasant result of a driver running into the back of a motionless auto, thinking he was in a travel lane. But I also grasped the meaning and context of the serious advice being offered: be sure you assess the potential of any apparent trends before you commit yourself and your resources in that direction. And then I took her counsel to another level. My outgoing nature will often reach out to someone who on the surface seems needy but whose underlying motives are questionable. I need to dig deeper to be sure I'm not getting into a spiritually unhealthy relationship. The Apostle Paul cautioned the Corinthians that "bad company corrupts good character."

2nd Peter 3:17: "Be on your guard so that you may not be carried away by the error of lawless men."

POWER FAILURE

*T*he electrical power grid in our suburban community is fairly modern. Most of the utility's infrastructure is below ground. As a result, we're less vulnerable to the types of widespread power failures that can cripple other areas of the Plains states during the storm season. That's not to say, however, that it never happens. Just this week, a construction worker at the site of a new subdivision accidentally – dare I say carelessly – sliced through an underground cable, plunging our neighborhood into darkness. Well, it was still daylight, so I could see to make my way around the house. But I couldn't use the stove, the laundry, the phone or the TV. Few things in my life are more frustrating than losing power. I wondered what would have caused our pioneer settlers similar frustration two centuries ago when electricity was unknown. And I certainly want to stay in intimate relationship with Jesus, my Savior, to avoid any failure of <u>that</u> power source.

1ˢᵗ Corinthians 18-19 "I pray that the eyes of your heart may be enlightened in order that you may know … his incomparably great power for us who believe."

QUILTS

—————— ❋ ——————

*A*re you a quilter? If so, I admire your artistry and detailed handwork. On our trips through Amish country over the years, I've been fascinated by the intricate designs created by that culture's women. In a weak moment, I spent a few dollars to buy one. It wasn't until we returned home that I looked closely at the quilt's flip side. It was easy to see the hand-tied knots that secured the interlocking designs on the front of the quilt, and the thread lines that trailed from one square to another. Even the back of the quilt had its own organized patterns, but they were humbly supporting the grandeur of the front side. I can't help but see similarities in our own lives together in God-inspired relationships. For some of us, our visible beauty is marred on the backside by raw knots and crisscrossing strings. For others of us, we're the flip side of the quilt: we're the invisible support system that quietly and lovingly holds it all together. Either way, God not only covers the raw backside with His grace, but also empowers the lowly to give brilliance to the quilt.

Matthew 5:5 "God blesses those who are humble, for they will inherit the whole earth. (NLT)"

FOCUS ON HEALING

―――――❋―――――

The list of major surgeries I've undergone over the years reads like a medical dictionary. I used to describe myself jokingly as a parts-missing turkey. After the first operation, I discovered I had a fairly high tolerance for physical pain. Through several surgeries that followed, I relied on that gift to help me focus on healing, and except for necessary dressing changes and infection control, I pretty much ignored the wound itself. Praise God – there were never any serious post-operative complications. By contrast, my tolerance for emotional pain is pretty low. I'm easily hurt by others' insensitive comments or their apparent indifference toward nurturing our relationships. My faith has led to me apply the same technique that successfully carried me through my physical ailments: focus on the healing, not the hurt. If I dwell on what it is, or who caused it, the wound gets deeper and more painful. Surrendering the wound to Jesus, the Great Physician, is the only way to promote complete recovery.

Acts 10:36-38 "… [Jesus] went around doing good and healing all who were under the power of the devil, because God was with him (v38b)."

LOVE

INVEST

*W*hen we invest in a financial opportunity, it's a decision made solely by us. Others may try to influence us, but at the end of the day we're the ones who choose what, or whether, to invest. God presents us with another kind of investment opportunity virtually every day: sharing ourselves with neighbors and co-workers. His Word commends us to embrace these one-on-one opportunities but the decision to invest in any of them rests squarely on our own shoulders. When we invest ourselves in others, claiming strength from the Holy Spirit, we realize a far greater return than we could ever find on Wall Street. Without being intrusive, find ways to get to know them better. Demonstrate sincere interest in their families, their work, their struggles. In doing so, we reflect Jesus' love and light into <u>their</u> lives, something they'll remember long after they're no longer neighbors or co-workers.

Luke 10: 25-37 "Love your neighbor as yourself." (v27b)

SPLINTERS

A few years ago I was struggling with a major crisis in my life. I found myself hanging on to whatever I could find to keep me focused on Jesus and the peace that only He could provide during that stormy time. On one particular day during that time, I stopped by my daughter's house. Once inside, I felt a sharp pain in my hand. I looked down, and was appalled to find I'd picked up a sliver. I realized it was probably the result of grasping the rustic wooden rail on her back steps. The image that popped into my mind at that moment was of Jesus' cross. I was holding so tightly to His cross during those days that I could literally feel the splinters of the crude wood. My friends, you need to cling to the cross of Jesus so fiercely that you get splinters!

1 Corinthians 1:18 "For the message of the cross…is the power of God."

CLEANING MY STOVE

❋

*A*s I was cleaning my stove top this morning, I realized some of the goo was older than I'd thought. If I'd spent just a few minutes wiping up spills right after they occurred, the exhaustive scrubbing I was now grunting my way through wouldn't have been needed. The same thing is true with our daily goof-ups and faux pas. Most of the time, they're not world class screw-ups. The problem is, unless we clean up the little messes as they happen, they tend to accumulate unwanted debris that even intense elbow grease won't dislodge. Self-esteem suffers, relationships get infected. Whether it's small or big, Jesus is the perfect "Brillo pad." No matter how dirty we feel, nor how burnt on the spill may be, a one-word prayer to Him will suffice: "Help!" With just a gentle touch of His hand, you're cleansed. And the cleansing is soul-deep.

Hebrews 10:19-22 "Let us draw near to God...having our hearts sprinkled to cleanse us."(v.22)

GRANDSON'S CALL

------------------------❋------------------------

*I*t's Christmas time here. In our family, we get all tingly and squishy thinking about how to honor each other with gifts that are outside the box (no pun intended) and yet useful. Sometimes that takes a little extra effort. One morning this week I took a phone call from one of my grandsons. He said he had a gift idea for Grandpa, and wanted my opinion. My heart melted; how cute was this! And then he asked, "What about you, Grandma? What would you like?" At that, I was on Rubber Leg Street! When I'd pulled myself together, I told him simply, "Just love me." I believe God wants a call from each of us, every day, asking Him what He would like us to give Him today. What a great prayer! "God, what can I do for You today?" And during that call, He expects us to let Him know what we need for the day. You know what? He'll answer us, if we come to Him in humility and faithfulness.

Proverbs 18:16 "A gift opens the way for the giver and ushers him into the presence of the great."

HEART REPAIR

---❋---

*E*very once in a while, I struggle with what I've diagnosed as a hardened heart. Thankfully, it's not an everyday thing. But, like the migraines that overtake me occasionally, I can sense when the "hard heart syndrome" is approaching. It's characterized by the onset of negativism and criticalness. So this morning I decided to ask God to take a look at my heart. Symbolically, I took it from my chest and handed it to Him. I said it needed some repairs... some restoration and fine tuning. It feels very crusty in some areas, and needs some sanding and filing to make it softer. It feels like it's calloused! I told Him I could leave it with Him while He fixed it, because I know He has lots of customers. He said, "I'll fix it while you wait." While I waited, I was able to pray for family, friends, other things. When it was ready, He put it back in just the right place. He gave me the gift of peace. Go to God with your crusty heart. Talk to Him and be still with Him. He will do the rest.

Psalm 51:10-12 "Create in me a clean heart, oh God. (v.10)"

LAUGHTER

*G*od loves to hear us laugh. Laughter lifts our spirits. Recent medical research tells us laughing with friends releases feel-good brain chemicals called endorphins, which also relieve pain. When my family gets together, inevitably there is laughter. This Thanksgiving, as we sat around the table after a great meal, somebody put the palm of his hand to his mouth, exhaled sharply – and (please excuse the frankness here) it sounded just like flatulence. We all laughed. That was the cue for group competition, trying to outdo each other. We heard the sounds of a weed-whacker, a speed boat, a motorcycle, more flatulence, and more guffawing. One of my grandsons asked, "Why does this happen only at Grandma's? Lots of laughter, crazy stuff like this?" And one of my sons-in-law thoughtfully offered, "Could it be because Jesus is here in this place?"

Psalm 126:2-3 "Our mouths were filled with laughter." (v.2a)

GENERATIONS

*O*ne of the "do-overs" in my life would be to go back to school and acquire a Doctor of Psychology degree. I'm fascinated with trying to figure out why folks around me do what they do. My kids joke about "hanging out my shingle." A component of my amateur psychological evaluation is the family's genealogy. Or, in my own words, "Apples don't fall far from the tree." At a more significant level, there's value in considering how our ancestors have brought us to where we are today. We can benefit from their failures and successes, and share those experiences and lessons to grow and encourage the next generation after us. In its most basic form, the Holy genealogy culminates in Jesus' birth, death and resurrection so that we can experience His grace and eternal life with Him in Heaven. And, as you read deep into the New Testament, you grasp how God calls you to share this same holy transformation with everyone in your "Jesus family." I'm struggling with the ageing process, but I hear God tell me, "You're the messenger!""

Deuteronomy 6:7: "Teach them repeatedly to your children. Talk about them while sitting in your house or walking on the road, and as you lie down or get up."

KITCHEN RECIPE

*T*have a cutting board in my kitchen that describes a "Recipe for a Woman of Faith." I bought it quite some time ago, and unfortunately can't attribute the source. But it's worth repeating here.

"Start with a spirit reverent and still. Add in prayer to follow God's will.

"Mix with trust and then let rise with Scripture, powerful and wise.

"Blend with loving, righteous living. Season well with deep thanksgiving.

"Pour in praise from a heart that's true. Yield: one woman of faith...that's you!"

Proverbs 31: 10-31 "She watches over the affairs of her household and does not eat the bread of idleness." (v.27)

THANKFULNESS

*O*ur family was together for dinner at our place on Thanksgiving eve. That in itself is something to be thankful for. In this era of global conflict and a variety of domestic stresses, family unity is increasingly scarce. The disconnect could be the result of a family member away on military service or – God forbid – a life sacrificed as a result. Or it could be irreconcilable marital discord. Whatever the reason, relational issues within the family are stressful – to say the least. So, back to our dinner. As we always do at this particular meal, everyone is invited to offer a specific reason for thanks. We took turns around the table. If we're honest with ourselves, there are myriad reasons to thank God for His provision. Without hesitation, my 10-year-old granddaughter said she was thankful for a roof over her head. How simple, I thought. It's something many of us take for granted…an everyday blessing, if lost for whatever reason, would be noticed immediately. Thank God for the simple things — and the honesty, innocence and spot-on insight of kids!

Psalm 150:6 "Let everything that has breath praise the Lord."

TRUST

————————✳————————

*M*y favorite Bible passage reads: "Trust in the Lord with all your heart, and lean not on your own understanding. Acknowledge Him in <u>all</u> your ways, and He will make your paths straight (emphasis mine)." I claim it every day, not only to remind myself of His great promise, but also to challenge myself to do just that – trust Him in all things. Some days it's difficult to live in that trust. My husband is having some unexpected – and I trust temporary – health issues right now. We have a wonderful doctor, and the medicines he's prescribed are the best available. But these resources are accessible only within the limits of physical science as conceived by human minds. On a daily basis, I'm seeking to find ways to trust God more and more, in all dimensions of my life. And as I spend time in His Word, I realize I have yet to learn the full depth of assurance that comes from accepting His invitation to trust Him in all things. Bottom line: He is all we really have.

Proverbs 3:5-6 "Trust in the Lord with all your heart…(v5)"

GRACEFUL

———————※———————

*A*s a Christmas gift, a friend gave me a jar candle. It's not a really big one. It's just the right size to sit by my sink and give off a soothing rice blossom aroma when I light the wick. Printed in large letters along the curved side is the word "graceful." Smaller letters define the word, and give an example of its use in this sentence: "Graceful souls dance through life with dignity and charm." You know what? Whenever I glance at the candle jar, my first reaction is to read the word as "grace-filled." That's where I am in my faith. I am filled with God's grace because I've accepted Jesus as my Savior. And then it's a short walk from there to the word "grateful" – grateful for what God has done for me through the death and resurrection of His Son, Jesus. Not to mention God's gift of grace – undeserved forgiveness of my human sinfulness. Or as someone has written based on the acronym GRACE, "God's riches at Christ's expense." Isn't that a wonderful aroma to inhale every day?

John 1:15-17 "And from His fullness we have all received, grace upon grace."

CHRISTMAS WITH FRIENDS

❄

*I*t's been an up-and-down Christmas season for us this year. One of the "up" times was an impromptu get-together with two of our favorite couples. The guys are as different as night and day. One is a big, loveable bear of a man who oversees maintenance and repair of dozens of pieces of heavy construction equipment for a well-known site contractor. The other is a laid-back top executive with one of the country's leading providers of industrial gases who'd give you the shirt off his back if you were in need. Their wives are part of my Snowflakes group. Because I'm at least 20 years their senior, this type of special friendship is all the more unique. Laughter, good food, good wine, heart-to-heart conversation…and Christmas. What better time to refresh our friendships and share traditions. It's also the time to renew and reaffirm our relationship with Jesus Christ. He is our Friend above all friends, and the manger calls us to His birthday party today and every day.

Luke 2:11 "Today…a Savior has been born to you; he is Christ the Lord."

HENRY

*E*ach of my five grandchildren is an inspiration to me. Because this collection of devotional thoughts is based on inspirational moments over my lifetime, I want to be sure I include the grandkids. As I write this, their ages range from 23 to almost 5. At 13, Henry is right in the middle. But that doesn't mean he's "average." Far from it. If his parents have had his IQ assessed, I'm not aware of it. No matter – I'm convinced he's close to the "genius" rating. When he was a fourth grader, he and a friend created YouTube videos using computer-generated stop-action photography. And now he's building his own computer. Did I tell you he's only 13? He's gifted in truly unique ways. Henry's an example of how God has built His church on earth. He created each of us as a unique, one-of-a-kind human being, but all created in His likeness. And each of us is gifted in special ways to build up His church. What's <u>your</u> gift? How are you using it to enrich His kingdom?

Romans 12: 5ff "Since we have gifts that differ according to the grace given to us, each of us is to exercise them accordingly (v6a)."

CHRISTMAS GIFTS

———————— ❋ ————————

*I*magine Christmas at your house. You're sitting around the tree with the rest of your family. The gifts have been handed out; they're piled at each person's feet. You know you have presents, but you've no idea what's inside those beautiful packages until you unwrap them. Our pastor told us this story at our Christmas Eve service: "My son would always shout 'Just what I wanted!' when he opened the toys and the electronic stuff. But when he opened Grandma's knitted afghan, the shout was barely audible. Years later, when the toys and gadgets had long since gone to the attic, it was Grandma's afghan that he still snuggled with at night." God's Christmas gift to us is Christ Jesus. Sure, we know the story about the manger and the shepherds and the Wise Men. But unless we reach out for it and unwrap it as our own, it will be nothing more than a pretty package under the tree. Open that package and open your heart, claiming Christ as God's gift of forgiveness and eternal life for you. The gift of His peace? It's just what you've always wanted!

John 14:27 "Peace I leave with you; my peace I give you…"

ROLE REVERSAL

*A*s parents, my husband and I have always felt the need to watch over our two daughters. Certainly that was our responsibility as they were growing up. We still hovered as they moved into adulthood, getting married and starting their own families, although (in <u>our</u> opinion, not necessarily <u>theirs</u>) more in the background. Thinking back, I realize my parents were the same way, easing back from their primary roles as I matured, but always there in the shadows – ready to leap into the breach when needed. Now that my husband and I have become "seasoned citizens," I recognize there was a neutral zone, so to speak. I can't pinpoint the years it started and ended, but it was kind of like "suspended parental animation." We were there on stand-by duty, but the call to action rarely came. Fast forward to this past year, when my husband and I made unrelated trips to the local ER. Both times, our daughters were right there by our side, loving us, supporting us, praying for us. At our age, this dramatic role reversal is the new normal for our extended family unit. May God grant them the grace to do for us what we did for them.

Ephesians 6:2 "'Honor your father and mother' – which is the first commandment with a promise – "

SWEETHEARTS

*M*y husband and I knew each other casually long before we were married. He grew up in New England and I in a Midwest college town. Both our families belonged to a small Baptist denomination with churches scattered across the country. We both attended the same national youth rally each year as high schoolers, and we would say hello. Looking back, we've confessed to each other we wondered "what if" – but at the time we each had our own puppy-love connections. After I graduated from high school, it seemed natural I'd attend college in my hometown. Would you call it Divine Intervention? Because the college had ties to our church denomination, this guy enrolled there as well — from halfway across the country! We ended up as biology lab partners our freshman year; he asked me out for Homecoming that fall…the rest, as they say, is history. What's my point? You may have a casual acquaintance with Jesus, but haven't yet made a serious commitment that can bring immeasurable lifelong blessings – not to mention salvation. The next time you cross paths with Him, let it happen!

2 Peter 3:9 "The Lord …is patient toward you, not wishing for any to perish but for all to come to repentance."

MEET A NEED

---- ❋ ----

*I*ndustrialist Henry Kaiser is quoted as saying, "All we have to do is find a need and fill it." To this day, budding entrepreneurs have hung their fates and fortunes on the ability to figure out what people want, and then find a way to satisfy that want. On a much more personal level, I try to live by the motto, "If you see a need, meet a need." I admit there are times I'm distracted by my own worries. But God calls me to be tuned in to what's happening in the lives of people around me. Proverbs 21:13 says, "He who shuts his ear to the cry of the poor will also cry himself and not be answered." I look for ways to encourage them, even help them in a modest way with material needs they may have. Sometimes it's nothing more than buying mac and cheese for my church's food bank. At the very least, I'm moved to pray for the spiritual needs of people around me. That's a need <u>everyone</u> has – and it costs you nothing to offer them prayer.

Philippians 2:4 "Do not merely look out for your own personal interests, but also for the interests of others."

JACOB

———————— ✳ ————————

*J*acob is the oldest of my five grandchildren. At this writing, he's 23. I find that hard to believe. It seems like just last week he was still in diapers and learning to walk. It's been fun to see him grow and mature into a solid young man who's trying to make his way in the adult world. One of my favorite Christmas memories of him was the year I gave him a huge toy semi-trailer – with a battery-powered air horn and diesel engine sounds. Toddler Jake would punch the "repeat" button until we all were laughing hysterically. Later, as a teen he was a high school basketball standout (with his father as his coach), and then excelled as a pitcher for his college baseball team. My prayer for him is that God will guide his steps so that the road will continue to be smooth and straight for him.

1st Peter 2:2 "Like newborn babies, crave pure spiritual milk, so that by it you may grow up in your salvation."

ONE WORD

*M*y good friend Lynn has challenged me to pick one word that would serve as my personal theme for the next 365 days. She forwarded me a link to the 12/31/15 blog of Margaret Feinberg, who offered examples of <u>her</u> previous years' words. They included JOY and FUN. It didn't take me long to accept Lynn's challenge, nor did it take me very long to choose the word TRUST. I definitely want to learn to trust God more. My desire is to trust Him completely, but the reality is I'm a lot like you. When the world pushes back hard, I waver. So not only do I <u>want</u> to trust, I need to understand <u>how</u> to trust. My visual here is the football quarterback who hands the ball to the running back – and then is powerless to do more. He simply trusts the play will work. In the past few days, I've been presented with major relationship issues far beyond my control. All I can do is hand them to God, and trust He'll handle them. Amazing! He's already resolved some of them.

Proverbs 3: 5-6 "Trust in the Lord with all your heart…and He will make your paths straight."

PITY PARTY

*G*od wants to hear my gripes. In fact, He actually begs me to share them with Him. Odds are, no one else is willing to offer the same invitation. At different times in my life, I've had "pity parties." I've even sent out invitations, but the only one who shows up is me. When I continue to talk about myself and my wounds, my friends and family are going to gradually shut me out. People aren't going to want to be around me if I whine all the time. I need to look within myself and figure out what that wound is, where it's coming from. God is the perfect listener — and the perfect healer. When I lay my hurting heart before Him in prayer, He not only hears me but He heals me.

1st Peter 5:7 "Give all your worries and cares to God, for He cares about you."

MANAGING YOUR HOME

───────── ✳ ─────────

*W*ho's the manager of your home? The Kendrick Brothers have produced a remarkable series of Christian movies, including "Fireproof," "Courageous," and perhaps the best known, "Facing The Giants." I've just finished watching their latest called "War Room." It portrays a husband and wife whose marriage is facing severe stress – and the God-loving woman who makes it her mission to coach the young wife into the role of a prayer warrior. It reminded me of my need to always be alert to the potential for Satan's attacks on my own marriage. And it made me wonder about who's the <u>real</u> manager of my grown daughters' homes, as well as the homes of my many friends and extended family. We need to remember who the enemy really is. Scripture is clear: Satan wants to steal, kill and destroy (John 10:10) – especially marriages. Listen to me, people. We are fighting the devil, not our spouses. God's there, waiting for us to offer up fighting prayers to Him.

James 5:16 "The prayer of a righteous man is powerful and effective (v16b)."

SERVANTHOOD

*M*y mother died in 1986 at the age of 70. My brother's close friend – and business associate at the time – was a beloved and silent servant during those days of grieving. His name is Jonathan. How's that for a not-so-coincidental association with their friendship connection (1st Samuel 18:1; also 1st Samuel 20)? Every morning until after the funeral, he'd let himself in my parents' front door with donuts and the paper, put on a pot of coffee, and then sit quietly in a corner of the living room watching for our family's further needs. He never asked if he could; he just did it. My friend Lynn does that today. She senses a need and then meets it, without asking. Bringing a meal to the house, sitting with me in the waiting room. Both examples of how Jesus calls us to selfless servanthood.

Psalm 103: 20-21 "Praise the Lord…you His servants who do His will (v21b)."

COMPASSION

-------------❈-------------

*M*ax Lucado tells the story of a man injured in a fire, whose face was burned and disfigured: "He wouldn't let anyone see him, including his wife. When she went to a plastic surgeon for help, the doctor assured her that he could restore her husband's face. But she wasn't there to restore her *husband's* face. She wanted *her* face disfigured so she could share in his pain." When I heard this story, I was reminded in a powerful way how Jesus knows our every pain and anguish. He came to earth in human form so that He could experience all that we, as humans, endure in this earthly life. As a result, His compassion is real. When He tells us He knows how we feel, and how we struggle, He means what He says. When He challenges us to bear one another's burdens, it's not just lip service. He's been there Himself, and He knows how it feels.

John 1:14 "The Word became flesh and made his dwelling among us."

NORAH MAE

---❋---

*S*he's my first granddaughter. One of many reasons I love her is because her middle name is the same as mine. Of my five grandchildren, she checks in at number four. In her own primary family she's the middle child, with an older brother and younger sister. Within the tapestry of the world at large, she's almost invisible. She's quiet, laid back, and rarely demanding. Yet her heart, as I see it, is huge. Without reservation, she demonstrates her love for her family with hugs, and more hugs. Her warm, welcoming personality has attracted lots of school friends her own age. She enjoys helping fellow students when she perceives them in need. She seems to have a sixth sense about that. She's already won a Pillar of Citizenship Award from her school. At the moment, she's in fourth grade. Lord willing, I'll still be around to see how or what she chooses as a life work when she's older. I'm betting it will be some sort of serving role, making a quiet but significant difference in the lives of folks in need.

Philippians 2:3-5 "Do nothing out of selfish ambition or vain conceit. Rather, in humility value others above yourselves (v3)."

PAYOFFS

My husband and I have been blessed over the years by our relationship with a Godly pastor who knows what it's like to deal with addictions and perennial behavioral issues. He's confessed to us that his own issue has been his dependence on approval and perfectionism. At one time, as the co-pastor of one of the Midwest's largest and fastest-growing televised congregations, he says he was more consumed by the need for affirmation and leading a "perfect worship production" than he was leading people to Christ. I love him for his candor, and how he's been a powerful witness to us. He's helped us understand how unhealthy behaviors often produce a shallow payoff that not only rewards us for that behavior but also keeps us repeating that behavior to generate that payoff. To paraphrase Albert Einstein's definition of insanity: repeating the same negative behavior over and over, expecting a different result.

2 Timothy 1:7 "For God has not given us a spirit of fear and timidity, but of power, love, and self-discipline."

GRIEVING

———————— ❉ ————————

$\mathcal{L}$ately I've found myself grieving other peoples' losses people I don't even know! Maybe I've done it subconsciously for a long time, but it's only recently that I've become aware of the experience. I heard a news story of a family in Texas who lost a loved one in a bizarre accident. I found myself crying. Then a high school student in the town next to us committed suicide, and I found myself crying. Within the past week, one of presidential candidate Ben Carson's campaign volunteers died in a car wreck here in Iowa. I found myself not only crying, but sobbing – for the young life lost, and for Dr. Carson's grief as he suspended his campaign to be with the bereaved family. I'm OK with discovering this new dimension of my emotional tool kit. God created me with a soul that mirrors the hurts of folks around me, as well as in distant places. I love Him, and He calls me to express my empathy for others.

Galatians 6:2 "Carry each other's burdens, and in this way you will fulfill the law of Christ."

SABBATH REST

*M*y husband and I grew up in families tied to an agrarian Sabbatarian Baptist denomination (Seventh Day Baptist). Within that tradition, we understood God's grace is free to all who believe. But we were also taught, out of loving response to Him, we should honor His commandments, including keeping the Sabbath day holy. Our upbringing defined Saturday as that Sabbath. As we've moved over the years, we've drifted away from home churches and their support systems that made Sabbath observance "convenient." Along with hectic work and family schedules, with their secular emphasis, honoring a Sabbath concept has been difficult. Here in Iowa, where agriculture defines the economy, I wistfully reflect on Old Testament tenets related to the Sabbath, including this one from Leviticus 25: "For six years you shall sow your field, and for six years you shall gather in its produce. But in the seventh year, the land shall have a complete rest, a **Sabbath** to the Lord." Agronomists say it makes great sense.

Exodus 34:21 "Six days you shall work, but on the seventh day you shall rest. In plowing time and in harvest you shall rest."

BENJAMIN

*M*y second oldest grandson Ben is 19. His mother, our older daughter, may have given little thought to the Biblical genealogy embracing his name. But it intrigues me to discover it includes the Old Testament's King Saul and the prophet Jeremiah, as well as the New Testament's Apostle Paul. Of similar interest to me is that after the Old Testament division of the Promised Land, the tribe of Benjamin was the buffer zone between Israel and Judah. Does Ben have any sense of this Biblical history? I doubt it. What I do see in him is a huge heart for everyone he knows. He is loving, kind, and considerate. Right now he's attending a community college and working, very hard with great focus, in a franchised fast-food restaurant. I'm excited to see how this all will work out for him, and how and when he'll come to see God's life-plan for him. His name literally means "son of My right hand."

Colossians 3:12-17 "Therefore, as God's chosen people, holy and dearly loved, clothe yourselves with compassion, kindness, humility, gentleness and patience (v12)."

ELIGIBLE RECEIVERS

---------------- ✳ ----------------

*N*ext weekend we'll be watching the Super Bowl. That's why I thought of this title. And as I spend time in the four Gospels, I'm awestruck at the diversity of "eligible receivers" whom Jesus touched during His time on earth. Zondervan's NIV Life Application Study Bible is my favorite scriptural resource. I love the footnotes. On the topic of eligible receivers, one footnote asks, "Whom did [Jesus] consider important enough to touch?" The list was endless: a hated tax collector, a Roman centurion, an adulteress woman, political leaders, a criminal, a king, an insane man, a housewife, a traitor... The footnote continues, "Jesus cares equally for all. No person is beyond the loving touch of Jesus." Where would you rank yourself right now on a continuum of reputation, wealth, position or social status? Jesus' arms are long enough and strong enough to hug you to Him now and forever.

Romans 5:8 "But God demonstrates his own love for us in this: While we were still sinners, Christ died for us."

ENCOURAGEMENT

❋

*U*nique, clever, beautiful, useful: words that describe the handmade note cards that my dear young friend delivers to me in great quantities. I don't know how Kari does it. She's a second grade teacher with a passion for addressing the needs of each one of her two-dozen-plus students. She's a great mom to two young sons. She's a devoted wife of a local restaurateur. On top of it all, she turns out oodles of these marvelous handmade, one-of-a-kind note cards. This creative gift of hers supports my own gift of sending words of encouragement to people far and wide. Kari gives me the decorated blank page; God gives me the specific sentences or phrases to write to someone I've heard is in need of encouragement. I guess you might describe us as a perfect team, Kari and me. She provides the platform, I do the rest. You can do it too, even if you don't have Kari's cards. Know of someone struggling? Find a way to let that person know you care.

Romans 12:6-9 "We have different gifts…if it is to encourage, then give encouragement…"

LEGACY

*T*had two friends who died many years ago. It could be that neither of them knew this, but in my eyes they both played a major role in guiding me and encouraging me in my faith walk. To this day I have vivid memories of their words of wisdom when we would talk about Jesus. They never faltered in pointing the pathway to trusting in the grace of God and the forgiveness and eternal life available through the death and resurrection of His son, Jesus. At the very least, my hope is that this series of devotional thoughts will spur just one person "out there" to confess Jesus as Lord. But more than that, for you believers reading this, I pray that you will be the ones to lead others to Him. He calls you to leave a legacy of love. Do it now. Do it right. Do it right now!

Mark 10:45 "For even the Son of Man did not come to be served, but to serve, and to give his life as a ransom for many."

NEGATIVITY

*O*ne of my spiritual struggles is with not only being critical of situations or people, but also the negativity that follows. When I begin to experience those thought patterns, it's usually because I've allowed myself to focus way too much on what's bad in my life. Hey, folks, let's be honest with each other. Life this side of Heaven has its junk. We've created some of it as a result of our own choices. Some of it just happens without any contributions from us. But, thanks to God, we're not locked in to self-talking about just the trash. God tells us in Scripture that we have the mind of Christ (1st Corinthians 2:16). Let's put that Holy Mind to work, and change our thinking. My process is to start listing each gift, each blessing, God has given me over the years. Scripture promises that when I align my thoughts with God's, His peace will protect my thoughts and my heart.

Philippians 4:7 "Then you will experience God's peace, which exceeds anything we can understand. His peace will guard your hearts and minds as you live in Christ Jesus."

SERVANTHOOD 2

❋

*A*unt Margaret was my favorite. People who didn't know her well thought she was kind of gruff. But I knew she had a heart of gold, and would do just about anything for someone in need. She was a hard worker, doing what she could to help make ends meet for her husband and their two adopted children. Besides juggling a homemaker's busy schedule, she drove a school bus mornings and afternoons. She took in laundry (as a kid I remember seeing it hung indoors over a large furnace grate set in their dining room floor). And she gave "home permanents" to women in her circle of friends, taking little or no pay in return. Her favorite hymn was "In The Garden," which tells of walking and talking with Jesus. She died unexpectedly a month before my wedding, where she was to have cut the cake. Years later, I still miss her. But I am absolutely confident I will see her again in Heaven (*see 1ˢᵗ Thess.4:17*). Maybe we can cut cake together!

Psalm 116:15 "Precious in the sight of the Lord is the death of His saints."

SUPER SALE

---❋---

We're in mid-February, and all of my favorite mall stores are having Presidents' Day sales. Here's the thing: when I'm shopping for cosmetics or personal clothing, I tend to go when I <u>want</u> to. But when I need stuff for the household, like linens, I watch for the "year's biggest sale". We women love sales! Sorry; I mean, we woman do rationalize, as in "it's okay to spend money, because it's 'on sale'". So I needed a set of king-sized sheets for our bed. At regular prices, they're extremely expensive. But I got what I wanted for an awesome sale price. I'm so glad God doesn't wait until I'm tagged with a sale price before He decides to redeem me. From Genesis to Revelation, the Bible assures me He believes I'm worth full price – the death of His Son Jesus on the Cross to wipe out my sins, and Jesus' resurrection from the grave to confirm my eternal salvation.

John 10:10 "I have come that they may have life, and have it to the full."

UNWRAPPED GIFTS

———————※———————

The more I'm in the Word – not just reading Scripture but also pondering it and figuring out, with the Spirit's guidance, how it applies to my life – the more I realize how much I and the folks close to me have been missing. To be sure, many of us have missed the "bottom line:" salvation is God's gift if we will only trust Him and accept His grace (undeserved forgiveness of our human failures). Much more than that, though, are the unknown numbers of very specific gifts that we've failed to experience because we've not been tuned in to God's "game show channel". I've come to view this as a series of presents attractively wrapped and tagged with our names that sit on shelves in a closet. God's waiting for us to connect with Him in special ways so that we can claim our packages, not only to enjoy but also to apply those gifts while we're still here on Earth.

James 1:17 " Every good and perfect gift is from above, coming down from the Father of the heavenly lights, who does not change like shifting shadows."

VALENTINE

In today's commercial world, Valentine's Day has become (or was it "created as"?) an opportunity to express your love to a spouse, children, grandchildren and friends. We send them a heart card, give them a small gift, or remind them face-to-face how much we love them. I spent some time learning about the life of the early church's real Saint Valentine. You should too; it's a remarkable story. He was martyred in 269 AD for encouraging young couples to marry within the Christian church. A Roman Catholic prayer to Saint Valentine reads, in part: "Some loves are fleeting, but that which is built on You will never fail." God is the You in that prayer. He doesn't set aside just one day a year to love you or to call you to love Him. His love for you is 24/7, and He desires you to love Him the same way. His Valentine card to us is the Holy Bible, the world's most perfect love letter.

John 3:16:"For God so loved the world that he gave his one and only Son, that whoever believes in him shall not perish but have eternal life."

WALMART

*J*erry and I do our twice-a-month grocery shopping at Walmart – at least for the majority of our pantry's needs. It's become part of our routine. I'm sure you know what it's like grocery shopping: you're the one going in the right direction down each aisle, and everyone else is swimming upstream toward you. Battling that traffic gives me a perfect chance to eyeball the tremendous cultural diversity surrounding me – not only in the store, but in our larger community. In 1975, Iowa's then-governor Bob Ray led the way in welcoming Vietnam's Tai Dam immigrants, and later the "boat people." Since then, our state's open arms have received thousands of other nations' refugees escaping war, hunger and oppression. As I pass them in the Walmart aisles, I wonder if they know Jesus. Without doubt, this is the "harvest" He talks about in Scripture (John 4:35). What am I doing to make sure I'm one of the field hands?

Luke 10:2 "The harvest is plentiful, but the workers are few. Ask the Lord of the harvest, therefore, to send out workers into his harvest field."

FAITH

*P*eriodically I need to remind myself that what some-times looks like an obligation is instead an oppor-tunity to serve – and be enriched in the process. Such is the case with my weekly Thursday noon hour with my youngest grandchild Faith. She has just turned 5, and next fall will enter kindergarten. But this school year, I've been picking her up once a week at her morning pre-K, spending 45 minutes with her in my car while she eats her sack lunch, and then dropping her off at a different afternoon pre-K. This, while her mother works her part-time job. Sometimes before I head out for the pick-up, I do the woe-is-me dance. And as soon as Faith is in the car, that all changes. I'm infected with her simple joy and exuberance, and regaled with the latest family doings – including tales her mom might not want me to hear! I'm serving my daughter and granddaughter, getting to know both Faith and God better – because she's created in His image.

Matthew 19:14 Jesus said, "Let the little children come to me, and do not hinder them, for the kingdom of heaven belongs to such as these."

BRAND NEW DAY

---❊---

"Thank you for a brand new day, a brand new chance to stand and say I love You. Help me find the words to say that tell you in a brand new way, I love You. Oh, how I love You, more than words can say, in the deepest heartfelt way, oh Lord how I love You." Those lyrics from Tommy Walker's praise song float through my brain many mornings, often before I've even brewed my first cup of coffee. Each new day is much more than a function of the clock or the calendar. It's a gift from God to allow us a fresh start, whether the previous 24 hours were productive or disruptive. And while our prayers for the most part are the same as yesterday's – for us, for our family, for our country, for forgiveness, prayers of thanksgiving – Jesus' life, death and resurrection give a new perspective to those prayers each day. The Cross makes each day a "brand new day" through Jesus' eyes. Don't miss it!

Lamentations 3:22-23 "His compassions never fail. They are new every morning; great is Your faithfulness!"

GOALS

$\mathcal{A}$fter 27 years as head boys' basketball coach at one of our metro area's high schools, our son-in-law Brad realized a life-long dream. He was offered and accepted the head coaching position at a small but prestigious college in central Iowa. He racked up a 398-213 record as a high school coach, winning 9 league championships outright and taking his team to 7 state tournaments. Despite that success, he never lost sight of his goal to coach at the collegiate level. And in his first year in that new role, he turned around a program that had struggled through five losing seasons and dwindling attendance. When he took over, he told his team his goal was simple: make it to the league's post-season tourney. On the shoulders of reinvigorated student support, they did just that. I've no idea whether Brad took his goals before God in prayer. But God tells us He'll bless our plans if we will bring them to Him in humility and trusting that they'll be aligned with His will for us.

Proverbs 16:3 "Commit your actions to the Lord, and your plans will succeed."

SOLID FOUNDATION

---✳---

*O*ur son-in-law Chris is an extremely gifted man. After spending several years in progressively responsible roles in city government as a leader in land use planning, he's now doing the same thing within a private consulting group with national clients. He demonstrates a similar leadership ethic within his primary family: his wife (our daughter) and their three young children. Here's one of the more obvious examples. Soon after their marriage, and before the arrival of their first child, he bought a small starter home – a bungalow — in an older neighborhood within their community. As the family grew, and largely with his own hands, he planned and then gradually built an addition that more than doubled the size of the home. When I peer into the large open basement underneath the addition, I can clearly see how much planning and effort went into making sure the footings and foundation walls were sound. Jesus challenges us to build our lives on a similar solid foundation – His Word.

Matthew 7:21-28 "Therefore everyone who hears these words of mine and puts them into practice is like a wise man who built his house on the rock (v24)."

STRING OF PEARLS

* * * ❊ * * *

A few years ago, my older daughter invited me to join her on a business trip she was making to Boston. It took me all of two seconds to accept. During her down time from the conference she was attending, we enjoyed wonderful food, awesome scenery, and loads of laughter. We share the same offbeat sense of humor, and laughter is always part of who we are when we're together. On this particular occasion, the "elevator scene" was the highlight of the trip. Sorry, my lips are sealed. During our stay, I bought a string of pearls from the hotel's gift shop as a souvenir of the trip. Now, whenever I wear them, I think of that very special time we had together. The Bible is like that. It's God's "string of pearls" that we can put on every day to remind us of who He is, how and why He loves us like He does, and how we can trust Him with every detail of our lives.

Psalm 119: 105 "Your Word is a lamp to my feet and a light for my path."

THE INVITATION

J'm pretty sure my husband's Rhode Island high school graduating class will be having its 55th reunion sometime this year. (I am NOT going to tell you which reunion <u>my</u> class will be having!) But since he's closed the e-mail account to which previous invitations were sent, and we have a new USPS address since the last reunion, it's possible we won't get a formal invitation. There's no doubt he'd be welcomed if he showed up anyway. But somehow that invitation paves the way and makes it all official. There are times when we wish someone would come to visit us, or even call us just to chat. We assume our friends know they're welcome to drop by or phone us at any time. When days go by and we've not seen or heard from them, we're disappointed. In all relationships, God calls us to initiate the contact. Take the lead, He says, and let Me be seen in your invitation to get together…to talk with one another… to be with each other in My house of worship.

Matthew 22:1-10 "Go to the street corners and invite to the banquet anyone you find (v9)."

1984

❋

*N*o, that is <u>not</u> a reference to George Orwell's futuristic novel. It's the year in which I finally surrendered my life to Jesus Christ. Even after the intervening years, memories of that time are still vivid. Our older daughter had just graduated from high school and was striking off on her own. But that was the least of the changes. My husband had just lost what he'd considered his ideal lifetime job as a senior executive with a large television group. And me? I was enduring painful, long-term radiation as a follow-up to my first mastectomy – and botched reconstructive surgery. Long story short: my husband moved to another city to find employment, we moved into divorce mode, and I moved into despair. Early one morning, I finally confessed, "God, I can't do this anymore on my own. I need You and Your Son Jesus at the center of my life." Instantly, I felt an unprecedented peace flow through my body, and heard God's reply: "Girl, I got this for you." Well, not quite verbatim, but I knew what He meant.

Romans 10:9 "If you declare with your mouth, 'Jesus is Lord,' and believe in your heart that God raised him from the dead, you will be saved."

BRIDGES NOT WALLS

---✳---

"*G*ood fences make good neighbors," wrote Robert Frost in his poem "Mending Wall." It was written while Frost lived on his family's farm in New Hampshire. My husband's a New England native, and appreciates the practicality of stone walls. They were the tangible result of the region's earliest settlers' efforts to clear the land for farming. As they prepared their acreages for the first plantings, they pulled rocks and stones from the dirt and piled them in an orderly line along their properties' boundaries. In his teens, my husband and his father roamed the back roads of Rhode Island looking for abandoned stone walls to "raid" for the backyard patio they were building. Once the project was done, they discovered there was a flat slate headstone that had inadvertently found its way into the terrace. But I digress. I can understand the logic of Frost's maxim if it has to do with respecting each other's possessions and personal space. On the other hand, it contradicts my Christ-centered concept of loving your neighbors so much you'll take extraordinary steps to reach out to them to strengthen relationships. The parable of the Good Samaritan is just one of many examples Jesus shared with His followers. Building bridges to restore broken relationships, and to establish new ones, is what Jesus teaches us throughout Scripture.

Ephesians 2:14 "For He Himself is our peace, who has made the two groups one and has destroyed the barrier, the dividing wall of hostility."

CONFESSION

I love the word <u>confession.</u> I totally appreciate that my Roman Catholic friends have an understanding of the word that includes sitting in a booth in anonymity, across a curtain from an ordained priest, owning up to one or more sins in order to be welcomed at the Eucharist. For me, it's a lot more basic than that. Over the years, I've developed an extra sense for knowing when I've strayed from God's will for my life. It's called a guilty conscience. When my daily prayer life starts to smell like days-old fish, I can conclude I've fallen short of His standards – and I need to clear the books. All I need to do is pray to Him for cleansing. Even though it's been a long time since a formal liturgy has been part of my worship experience, the words of King David as found in Psalm 51:10 still touch my heart: "Create in me a pure heart, O God, and renew a steadfast spirit within me."

1ˢᵗ John 1:8-9 "If we say that we have no sin, we are deceiving ourselves and the truth is not in us. If we confess our sins, He is faithful and righteous to forgive us our sins and to cleanse us from all unrighteousness."

TEAMWORK

---***---

*F*or the avid sports fan, March Madness means intense college hoops: wearing your favorite team's colors, hogging the TV remote on game day, and mourning/celebrating each bracket's outcomes. Here in Iowa, March Madness takes on an added dimension. Our high schools' girls and boys basketball teams work their way through post-season games with the goal of making the state tournament – a chance to play at "The Well" (Des Moines' Wells Fargo Arena, home of the finals). We've experienced that. As a high school coach, our son-in-law took his teams there several times. At any level, the game's success requires two major ingredients: a goal, and teamwork. In our spiritual life, the ultimate goal is to be with Christ in His heavenly home. His grace promises us we'll achieve that goal. But in response to the undeserved promise, He calls us – among other things – to contribute to the team. What am I doing to answer that call? Be part of a small life-group? Reach out to women less fortunate than me? Lead a Bible study?

<u>Romans 12:5</u> *"So in Christ we, though many, form one body, and each member belongs to all the others."*

EASTER

❋

My friend's son-in-law offered himself as a bone marrow donor for an unidentified recipient. One of his motivations was that his father, a leukemia victim who was scheduled for a similar transplant, died before the procedure could be arranged. That memory took my imagination a step further. Occasionally we hear news stories of a heroic act with a bittersweet ending: the trapped person was saved, but the rescuer, without comprehending the risk, died in the process. But what if a living organ donor knew beforehand that his or her gift would mean certain death? Or a rescuer knew he'd not survive the rescue? Jesus knew all along He would die on the cross to save me from myself. Yet He made that trip without hesitation. Would you do the same for someone you know?

Romans 5:7-8 "But God demonstrates his own love toward us, in that while we were yet sinners, Christ died for us (v8)."

A CHANGELESS GOD

———————— ❋ ————————

J'm so thankful that God never changes. His stead-
fastness shouldn't surprise me. After all, the
Scriptures put it quite simply: "Jesus Christ is the same
yesterday, today, and forever (Hebrews 13:8)." By contrast,
in this earthly life, relationships are dynamic. They're constantly changing. Not just between friends but also within
family. In another devotion, I talked about seasons of
friendships as sort of a natural ebb and flow. But there are
times when relationships are put on hold, even terminated
permanently, because of perceived wrongs. When I'm one
of the parties to the troubled relationship, I almost always
begin to wonder whether I was at fault. I'm not perfect,
but as often as not, after thinking it through, I realize I did
nothing to cause the rift. Yet God calls me to respond grace-
fully – reflecting His grace on the situation – rather than
strike back, isolate myself, or escape in any number of ways.
Model Christ as the healer, even if you weren't the hurter.
In the short run, it isn't easy. In the long run, if you take
the first step, crumbling friendships can almost always be
restored and become even more fulfilling.

*Luke 6:29: "If someone slaps you on one cheek, offer the other
cheek also. If someone demands your coat, offer your shirt also."*

EASTER CLOTHES

*O*ver the years my sense of appropriate attire for church worship has changed. A lot of that has had to do with the culture of the congregation where we've worshipped. For example, as a kid I was part of a conservative Baptist denomination where suits and ties were *de rigueur* for the guys, and dresses or skirts and blouses for women. Later, in another community as an adult, I felt comfortable in slacks and tennis shoes. And in still another congregation, in the summer, tee shirts and shorts seemed the norm. Get this: on a recent visit to my childhood church I noticed most worshippers were in jeans and casual tops. No matter where you're worshipping this Easter, you'll see folks decked out in their best and finest. Regardless of what you're wearing when you honor the Christ of the Resurrection, He sees you in your "robe of righteousness (Isaiah 61:10)".

2ⁿᵈ Corinthians 5:1-2 "For we know that when this earthly tent we live in is taken down …we will have a house in heaven, an eternal body made for us by God himself and not by human hands. We grow weary in our present bodies, and we long to put on our heavenly bodies like new clothing."

TV ADS

*T*hink I've been watching too much television lately? During my daily quiet time, my brain often starts to crank out TV commercials. Cue the trumpets, then the off-screen announcer: "Coming soon to your nearest church. Meet Jesus and learn the simple secret to eternal life." Or, "Life with Jesus in your heart is like biting into a Reese's peanut butter cup – you'll want more." Or, over sound effect of revving sports car engine: "From 0 to 60 in an instant…like God, always there when you call." Or (taking major liberties with the Mean Joe Greene Coca-Cola spot from the 1980 Super Bowl), "Jesus! Jesus! I just want you to know I think you're the greatest" "Thanks, kid. Catch my grace." Oh well, a person can dream, can't they?

1ˢᵗ Thessalonians 4:16-17 "For the Lord himself will come down from heaven with a commanding shout, with the voice of the arch-angel, and with the trumpet call of God. First, the believers who have died will rise from their graves. Then, together with them, we who are still alive and remain on the earth will be caught up in the clouds to meet the Lord in the air. Then we will be with the Lord forever."

B&W TV

---- ✳ ----

*A*s a kid, I'd walk to a friend's house to watch my favorite TV shows like Howdy Doody and Winky Dink & You. That is, until my folks bought their first television somewhere in the mid-1950's. All the programs, no matter what channel, were in black and white. Our entire family would sit and enjoy the shows, laughing, talking, eating popcorn and drinking homemade chocolate malts. Today, I have a big screen, high-definition, vivid color TV. But I still have fun dialing up those throw-back channels that are replaying what I call "rope operas" like Gunsmoke, Wagon Train, and Cheyenne in living black and white! The Bible – God's Holy Word – doesn't rely on high definition color or other fancy broadcast technology to convey its message of grace and salvation. From Genesis to Revelation, its black print on white paper is about as basic as it gets. What's more, we can – no, we <u>should</u> – replay it over and over to make sure we grasp and keep the message fresh.

1ˢᵗ John 5:11-12 "And this is the testimony: God has given us eternal life, and this life is in his Son. Whoever has the Son has life; whoever does not have the Son of God does not have life."

HEART CHECK

———— ✳ ————

J've come to realize that the Lenten season, especially culminating in Easter Sunday and Christ's resurrection from the dead, is like undergoing a cardiac evaluation. At least that's how I see it. Although I've had multiple health issues over the years, including two bouts with cancer, I praise God none of them have involved my heart. Oh, I've had EKG's once or twice, but only as part of routine exams. Nothing like cardiac catheterization, angiograms and similar high-end tests for heart disease patients. Here's my point: if ever there was a moment for me to pause and examine my heart – do I really believe, am I really a fully devoted follower of Christ – Easter is the time. The cross and the empty tomb make a great X-ray machine! And as one of my Bible study ladies so aptly put it, "If it weren't for Easter, Christmas would be just another birthday."

Jeremiah 17:9 'The heart is deceitful above all things and beyond cure. Who can understand it?"

TRADE-OFFS

※

*M*y sister-in-law is one of the most committed teachers I've ever met. She's a remarkable person who married young, raised three boys, and only then went on to college. She was relentless in pursuing her bachelor's degree, secured a second grade teaching job in her hometown – and then successfully completed her master's degree. She retired a year ago, and is aggressively moving into a new season of life. While she was teaching she was a pack rat, saving every possible clipping and teaching aid she thought valuable. Now, she's cleaning house. Not only is she giving away or tossing all those years' teaching materials, she's also adopted a novel approach to new acquisitions of household items. "If you're buying something new," she says, "you need to get rid of what it's replacing." In other words, she says, "you need to give up something to get something." When we accept Jesus Christ as our Lord and Savior, all we need to do is surrender to Him and ask Him to help us toss out the useless trash. He takes our past sins, and replaces them with the strength to be a new person in Him.

2ⁿᵈ Corinthians 5:13 "Therefore, if anyone is in Christ, the new creation has come: The old has gone, the new is here!"

HEAD TO HEART

---- ❋ ----

$\mathcal{M}$ercyMe, the contemporary Christian musical group, gave a concert at our church this past weekend. I didn't go to the concert, but I did get to hear them perform one song earlier that same evening at a packed Saturday night worship service. Both our daughters did have concert tickets. They said a highlight was the testimony of lead singer Bart Millard. He told the audience he'd been performing Christian music for 22 years, but it was only recently, as he put it, "that I finally got it." Or, as I like to say, "when you finally know that you know that you know." I wonder how many folks are merely intellectual Christians and haven't yet grasped the simplicity of faith. It saddens me that their knowledge of who Jesus is and what His death and resurrection means to them, hasn't made it yet from their head to their heart. It's in the heart where fact turns to faith and unshakeable belief.

Hebrews 11:1 "Faith is the confidence that what we hope for will actually happen; it gives us assurance about things we cannot see."

HEART REPAIR 2

*I*n another devotion titled "Heart Repair" I wrote about handing my heart to God for some fine-tuning. Since then, I've heard of the song "Tell Your Heart To Beat." It's been recorded by Danny Gokey as well as Phillips Craig & Dean, and perhaps others. I marvel at the story behind the song. It's said a famed surgeon performed a delicate operation on a woman's heart. At the end of the successful surgery, the woman's heart had ceased to beat. Although she was still under general anesthesia, the famous surgeon bent over her and, close to her ear, said very gently, "Mrs. Johnson, tell your heart to start beating again." Instantly, the repaired organ began a steady, normal pulsing. After a life filled with troubles and sorrows – or even when experiencing a one-time setback — we're left wondering to whom we can turn for healing. Jesus, the Great Physician, waits patiently for us to surrender to Him and His miraculous healing powers. When we do, He tells us we're restored to wholeness, and then He whispers, "Tell your heart to beat again."

Mark 1:32-34 "That evening after sunset the people brought to Jesus all the sick and demon-possessed. The whole town gathered at the door, and Jesus healed many who had various diseases."

INVEST & INVITE

---------------❋---------------

*W*hile preparing these devotional paragraphs for the publisher, I was going through some of the earlier drafts. The titles "Invest" and "The Invitation" caught my eye. I felt God's Spirit reminding me that the two concepts – invest and invite – are inseparable in His kingdom plan. When we experience His love and grace, we're compelled to <u>invest</u> ourselves in those around us. There's no more powerful way to let them know what God can do for them than by telling them what He's done for us! After that initial deposit, we're called to stay with them, mentoring them and encouraging them to take the same step of faith they've seen us make. That's the <u>invite</u> part of the process. Let me put it to you this way: I'm so excited about how God has saved me from my sinful past that I can't stop telling others about that rescue experience. Not only that, I want them to join me in the awesome Praise Party that goes on forever.

Matthew 28:16-20 "Therefore go and make disciples of all nations, baptizing them in the name of the Father and of the Son and of the Holy Spirit, and teaching them to obey everything I have commanded you."

SHATTERED GLASS

$\mathcal{I}$ grew up in a church with stained glass windows along the outside aisles, as well as behind the baptistry at the altar. And my husband's home church featured a 35-foot high stained glass rendering of Jesus "at the door knocking." For many of us, our lives now resemble those windows. We're cruising along day by day and suddenly we're brought to our knees by a glass-shattering life event. Each dimension of our life is represented by a different tint. The hundreds of multi-colored shards now scattered at our feet are painful reminders of what we used to be. And then Jesus is there, stretching out His arms to us, offering to put the pieces back together if we'll surrender to Him. The resulting spiritual artwork is a stained glass offering that literally calls out to the world around us that these kinds of repairs are available only at the throne of God's grace.

Jeremiah 18:1-6 "Like clay in the hand of the potter, so are you in my hand, Israel. (v6b)"

A CHILD'S PRAYER

————————— ❋ —————————

$\mathcal{I}$n his retirement years my brother Ron has taken to raising high-quality beef cattle. His son Dan does a great job of handling the day-to-day details of the operation. When one of their four-month-old heifers became pregnant, there was concern. What I know about animal husbandry you could put in a thimble with room to spare. But my quick research revealed the preferred earliest calving age for heifers is around two years. So, armed with this bit of critical information, I understood my brother's anxiety. As the young heifer was about to deliver, Ron's wife and a few grandchildren actually pulled up lawn chairs to watch. I guess you have to live on a farm to grasp the significance of all of this. As accustomed as she'd become to nature's ways among the herds, my sister-in-law felt she had to turn away. "Don't worry, Grandma," said 12-year-old Bella. "I asked God to take care of this." As adult followers of Jesus, we sometimes take prayer for granted. In this case, young Bella's calm confidence that God would hear and answer her prayer was especially assuring.

Luke 18:17 "Truly I tell you, anyone who will not receive the kingdom of God like a little child will never enter it."

CAREGIVER

❋

*M*y 49-year-old daughter is having a hip replaced next week. She had similar surgery five years ago. Her orthopod says the need for these operations at her relatively young age is probably due to her bone structure or high school basketball career – or both. As with her first operation, I'll be her primary caregiver for four weeks after she's home from the hospital. I consider caregiving among a mother's highest privileges. Yes, I know that helping her to bathe and shuffle to and from the toilet are among the many chores on my upcoming list. But I love her dearly and want to sacrifice myself for her in this time of need, especially when the pain of reconstruction is most intense. I can't help but draw the parallel with Jesus' sacrifice for us. He became our Supreme Caregiver through His death on the cross and His resurrection. He knows the pain we experience when we're betrayed by friends or because of our own screw-ups. He comes alongside us to comfort and reassure us that we'll be stronger through the healing He provides.

John 5:1-9 "Then Jesus said to him, 'Get up! Pick up your mat and walk.' At once the man was cured; he picked up his mat and walked (vv8-9)."

ROBE OF RIGHTEOUSNESS

---❊---

*T*like bathrobes. During those rare days when I have a few hours of down time, I enjoy lounging in my robe. The last one I had was a pink velour robe embroidered with a silk pink ribbon, acknowledging my victory over double breast cancer. The one I'm wearing now has vertical multi-color stripes, reminiscent of Joseph's "coat of many colors." At the moment, I'm caring for my daughter as she recuperates from hip replacement surgery. Today she complimented me on the robe, and we began talking about a variety of robes: choir robes, professors' robes, judges' robes, clergy robes. And then we moved on to a discussion of what the "robe of righteousness" might look like. Don't get me wrong. That special robe is reserved for each of us as we join God's heavenly choir at the Resurrection. I'm not there yet, but I'm sure looking forward to that day.

Isaiah 61:10 "I delight greatly in the Lord; my soul rejoices in my God. For he has…arrayed me in a robe of his righteousness…"

SQUANDER

————— ✳ —————

*W*hen we're not watching the Chicago Cubs baseball team on television, we're usually listening to their games on our kitchen radio. Pat Hughes, the Cubs' play-by-play announcer, is truly articulate. Like others who ply this unique craft, Pat's word pictures bring you directly into the ballpark and allow you to "see" what's happening at any moment. Today, at the end of an inning when the Cubs failed to score a run despite loading the bases, Pat offered this assessment: "Well, the Cubs squandered an excellent opportunity to take the lead." That word *squander* grabbed my attention, and I began asking myself, how many times have I squandered a chance to witness for Jesus Christ? If I were to be brutally honest, I know there are dozens of times when God created situations in which I could have told someone, in simple, easy-to-understand terms how much He loves them and how much He wants to have an intimate, grace-filled relationship with them. Father, forgive me for squandering those moments.

Colossians 4:5-6 "Be wise in the way you act toward outsiders; make the most of every opportunity. Let your conversation be always full of grace, seasoned with salt, so that you may know how to answer everyone".

TIDYING UP THE HOUSE

---❊---

*N*ot long ago I spent the weekend with my brother and his wife. They live six hours away from us, so it's a special gift to visit with them. While there, we went to church together. The pastor's message focused on the same theme written about by Robert B Munger when he penned "My Heart Christ's Home." I recommend that you read it sometime. You'll find it convicting! Anyway, the sermon I heard that day reminded me that Jesus waits patiently for us to invite Him into our hearts and lives. What He'll find once He crosses the threshold and stands in our vestibule may be household clutter that prevents Him from taking full occupancy. God's Word tells us that our sins are forgiven once we accept Jesus as our Savior. But for Him to move in permanently — and bring the total peace He promises — requires us to clean house. To borrow a popular TV commercial, with a slight twist, "What's in <u>your</u> closet?"

Ephesians 3:16-17 "I pray that out of his glorious riches he may strengthen you with power through his Spirit in your inner being, so that Christ may dwell in your hearts through faith."

TOP PRIORITY

---------- ❋ ----------

*J*t seems to me a devoted follower of Jesus Christ could easily find herself struggling to understand which of our Lord's commands and expectations take priority. All one has to do is spend time digesting His Sermon on the Mount (Matthew 5 through 7) to realize how many different behaviors He calls us to embrace. For me, the top priority is forgiveness. His final act, while suffering an agonizing death on the cross, was to forgive his critics and executioners. Right now I'm struggling with a couple of acquaintances who profess Christianity but whose daily actions seem self-centered. Neither of them has acknowledged my daughter's major surgery nor encouraged her in her recovery. I'm praying that the Holy Spirit will fill me with a real desire not only to overcome my being critical of these people but also to try to understand where they're coming from. And especially to forgive them, even though they don't know what they're doing. As Tony Dungy says in <u>Uncommon Life: Daily Challenges</u>, "Among Christians, less judgement means better relationships and more accomplishments for His kingdom."

Luke 23:24 Jesus said, "Father, forgive them, for they do not know what they are doing."

REFLECTING

---✳---

*M*y older daughter will be observing her birthday in about two weeks. And it's a big one. My first reaction to this pending milestone is a selfish one – it underscores how old <u>her mother</u> is! As her temporary caretaker over the past few weeks during her recovery from hip replacement surgery, I've had a chance to observe her more closely than usual. And I asked her what she's been thinking about as her birthday approaches. She replied, quite simply, "I've been reflecting." She didn't go into detail, and I sensed it wasn't a good time to ask her about those reflections. I know the combination of surgery and this not-so-welcome birthday have been tweaking her emotions big-time. And I know from personal experience there's only one direction you can look when you're lying on your back in a hospital bed: straight up. I just hope her reflections don't include major regrets. Her two sons are now adults, and in her mind "don't need me anymore." God calls us to rest at His feet and not only reflect on what He's done for us, but also to praise Him, worship Him and thank Him for those great gifts. Especially the gift of forgiveness through the love of His Son Jesus.

Psalm 46:10 "Be still, and know that I am God."

FINDING YOUR PURPOSE

---------------- ✳ ----------------

*O*kay, I know there are more than 60 Bible verses that warn about the consequences of a prideful heart. But at the moment, I can't help myself – and I'm trusting God will understand. I'm bursting with pride that, after rigorous auditions, our younger daughter has finally made the team: the praise team at our church. In my mind, that's quite an accomplishment. Several of the others on the team are professional musicians, and their vocal and instrumental contributions to our weekly worship are wonderful. Propelled by a special talent that allowed her to be a God-praising performer in school and as a church camp staffer, Sarah knew one of her callings was to share that talent as an adult. Now, at age 44, she's realized that dream. As I watched her on stage last weekend, before a congregation of 2000-plus, I saw my "baby bird" flying. Eyes closed and arms lifted in praise to her Lord, she was singing her heart out for God. When we use the gifts God's given us to honor and worship Him, we fly at the just right times in our lives.

Psalm 96:1-3 "Sing to the Lord a new song; sing to the Lord all the earth. Sing to the Lord, praise His name; proclaim His salvation day after day (vv1-2)."

PRAYER TIME

———————— ❈ ————————

I figured it was time to start praying for God's guidance about how – or even whether – to pursue publishing these devotions I'd been writing for this past year. It briefly crossed my mind that maybe I should have lifted up that prayer long before now. Oh well, here we are, nearly 200 titles later. When I'm feeling the need for serious, focused prayer time, invariably I'll kneel. I dropped to my knees yesterday to begin my prayer time. I had my prayer list, but God trumped it with His own agenda. It's amazing what God will reveal to you when you humble yourself before Him, on your knees, open to intimate two-way chatter. He showed me something I'd been harboring for a long time and in need of confessing. I covered my face in embarrassment and began confessing. I realized my daily busyness had blinded me to hidden sins that only His grace could cleanse. God is our <u>only</u> healer of heart issues. Friends, be zealous about your prayer time. And unless you're physically unable, do it on your knees!

Daniel 6:10 "Three times a day he [Daniel] got down on his knees and prayed, giving thanks to his God, just as he had done before."

SHAWL OF PRIDE

We live in the Des Moines, IA, metro area. One of the local attractions is the Iowa Hall of Pride, a venue memorializing our state's athletic, academic and political heroes. I'm sure other capital cities have similar exhibition halls. Lately I've been saddened by what I think I'm seeing as a "Shawl of Pride" that's draped around people whom I love. I'd never allow myself to speak to them about my observations. But what appears to be their self-centered attitudes and high opinion of themselves is getting in the way of their having a wholesome relationship with God. In many cases, the "shawl" may be perceived as a piece of Godly clothing, but in reality it masks who we really are: sinners in need of a Savior. The truth is we're a big zero without His saving grace. No matter our socio-economic status, when we confess to Him in prayer that we need Him, He replaces that "shawl" with His robe of righteousness.

1st Peter 5:5: "All of you, clothe yourselves with humility toward one another, because God opposes the proud but shows favor to the humble."

LEAVING HOME

You read about my grandson Jacob in a previous devotion. In case you forgot, he's the oldest of my five grandkids. And he's just now announced plans to "leave the nest" for the first time. Yes, I know he was away from home for months at a time when he was in college. But this is different. He's moving from Iowa to Arizona – as an adult, a professional, looking for the promise of initial career success. I have four other grandchildren, and I love each of them for their unique personalities and gifts. And I know I'm not Jake's mother, just his grandma. But, dog-gone it, it feels like I'm losing my own firstborn! Some of you reading this now have been there, and can relate. He's not sure what kind of opportunity he'll find, but he's going with that youthful confidence that there will be something there for him. I sense his excitement and the trust he has in himself to simply step out and go, with little concern for the risks. How exciting it would be for us as Christians to have that same confidence, to share Jesus with others without being afraid of the outcome. One thing for sure: Grandma will be praying for Jake every day, trusting that God will guard his heart.

Proverbs 4:23 "Above all else, guard your heart, for everything you do flows from it."

LUKEWARM

────────── ✳ ──────────

*U*ntil she was slowed by Alzheimer's, my moth-er-in-law did everything at full tilt. Long before she was widowed at age 75, she never let grass grow under her feet. Her college education was in the theatrical arts, and even though she never made the professional stage, she was always "on" whenever she had an audience. She had a big heart and loved everyone and everything. My kids were afraid to ride with her. She'd pull up to the stop sign at the end of her street and reach out her car window, directing oncoming traffic to let her through. At mid-day, on the spur of the moment, she'd declare, "Let's have a picnic!" Within minutes, she'd filled a basket with cream cheese and olive sandwiches, fixed a thermos of lemonade, and we'd head for her favorite parking spot at the beach. If she missed the thruway toll basket with her change, she'd simply wave and smile at the attendant and hit the throttle. And even after her husband died, it was still full speed ahead: "I need to take the old ladies to Monday Club!" Jesus wants us to demon-strate that kind of passion for Him and His Kingdom. In fact, He tells us in Scripture He'd rather know we were com-pletely cold toward Him than simply wishy-washy.

Revelation 3:15-16 "I know your deeds, that you are neither cold nor hot. I wish you were either one or the other. So, because you are lukewarm – neither hot nor cold – I am about to spit you out of my mouth."

MOTHER-IN-LAW

---❋---

*T*married an only child. Talk about a wake-up call! He was the joy of his mother's heart. Jerry was born and raised in southern New England and decided to enroll in a private college in Wisconsin. That's where we met on campus as freshmen, and had our first date that fall during Homecoming Weekend. We fell in love immediately. His mother seemed shocked that our relationship took root and blossomed so quickly. I came to learn later that she'd envisioned "her boy" attending an Ivy League school and marrying into the staid local social register. She and I had a few rough years early in our marriage. On our fifth anniversary, the card she sent us included a handwritten note addressed to me. She finally acknowledged I was the daughter-in-law she'd always hoped she'd have. It was God, not her, who chose me to be her son's wife. From that point forward, she and I got along famously. My advice to moms who are uptight about their young sons' future mates: in your daily prayers, include a petition that He will lead your boy to the Godly woman He's prepared for that special partnership.

Mark 10:7-8 "For this reason a man will leave his father and mother and be united to his wife and the two will become one flesh."

SAYING GOODBYE

---❈---

I invited my five-year-old granddaughter Faith to join me at our swimming pool today. She brought her mom along – probably because Faith won't be driving for at least another 11 years. She also brought her good friend Crosby. He's the same age as Faith. I didn't know it until we'd been in the pool together for a few minutes, but Crosby and his family will be moving tomorrow. Not just across town – across country. We're here in Iowa. He's moving to Colorado. Our own family has moved a few times, so I know a little bit about saying goodbye to friends we're leaving behind. I also remember a painful goodbye as a teenager, when my boyfriend and his family abruptly moved away. So today I'm wondering how five-year-olds say goodbye to each other. Faith isn't the only one losing a friend. Her mom – my daughter Sarah – is losing Crosby's mother as a close friend. As they left the pool I wished Crosby a good life. Looking back, that seems kind of empty. I should have commended him to the Lord by telling him Jesus loves him and He will protect him in his new home and life.

Matthew 19:14 "Jesus said, 'Let the little children come to me, and do not hinder them, for the kingdom of heaven belongs to such as these.' "

THE POOL

We live in a condominium complex with a beautiful swimming pool and adjoining clubhouse. The pool is surrounded by a broad concrete sundeck with a sheltering pergola at the shallow end. For each of the five summers we've been here, we've been privileged to invite immediate family members, friends, friends of family members, and visitors to join us poolside for swimming, sunbathing, and just plain relaxing together. This special amenity of our "home turf" is a gift that's brought together the folks we love for fun, sun and enjoying each other's company. It seems to me to be a fitting metaphor for the Living Water – Jesus Christ – who invites us to come to Him and enjoy the precious cooling and refreshment that only His love can provide. When we bathe in His life-giving water, we experience the unique refreshment, renewal, and reconciliation that He promises through His own baptism, life, death and resurrection.

John 4:14 "But whoever drinks the water I give him will never thirst. Indeed, the water I give him will become in him a spring of water welling up to eternal life."

HE'S GOT YOUR BACK

———————— ✳ ————————

I doubt an orthopedic surgeon would prescribe using a Bible as a back brace, but it sure worked for me at a time when I really needed it. It was early in 2012 and my husband and I were going through a difficult time. We were separated, and I was living temporarily with my daughters, their husbands and their families. During those weeks of emotional pain there were times when I felt incapable of even putting one foot ahead of the other. I would wake up in the middle of the night, open my Bible, and read from the Psalms. I found their words, their themes, even the rhythm of their poetry, especially soothing to my aching heart when I most needed it. I related to the Old Testament's King David (described as "a man after God's own heart" – see Acts 13:22), who wrote many of the Psalms, some during periods of anger, fear and grief. Each night when I finished reading, I would lie on my side and tuck my Bible into the small of my back before falling asleep, knowing God would protect me and that all would soon be well. I highly recommend it – spending time reading the Psalms, that is.

Psalm 4:8 "In peace I will lie down and sleep, for you alone, Lord, make me dwell in safety."

OBEDIENCE

---　✳　---

"*O*bedience" stirs a spectrum of emotions in folks, depending on what's going on in their lives when the word slaps them upside the head. For rebellious teenagers, obedience is the last thing on their minds. For adults who indulge in lawless behavior, obedience isn't even in their vocabulary. And for Christians who are faithful followers of Jesus, obedience to God's Word is the ultimate response toward self and others. For me, that last setting is where I am right now. For the past year I've been praying that God would show me a way to give Him as a gift to others. Why? Because of what He's done for me – and you get a tiny taste of those blessings in these pages. He answered my prayer by inspiring me to write these devotional vignettes. Here I am, a year later, writing, writing, writing — something I would NEVER have thought possible at age 72. At first, I was looking for simple ways to share these words with family and close friends. No way, God said; pray the Jabez prayer and let the messages in these pages go where God decides to take them.

1ˢᵗ Chronicles 4:10 "Jabez cried out to the God of Israel, 'Oh, that you would bless me and enlarge my territory! Let your hand be with me, and keep me from harm so that I will be free from pain.' And God granted his request."

FRIENDS

FRIENDS

---❋---

*T*here are days when I reflect on friendships I've had over the years. I find myself wondering why some have remained strong and others have faded. I think King Solomon's words regarding seasons (Ecclesiastes 3:1) apply to friendships as well as everything else "under the sun." Cross-country moves, job changes that interrupt special co-worker friendships, transitions in the other person's life, all help define the timeline of cherished relationships. I've also come to believe that even though the season of a certain friendship has come and gone, that person is always in my heart and head. A song on the radio…driving by our favorite diner…memories stimulated by casual conversation with other friends…bring past or distant friendships to mind. Michael W. Smith sings, *"Friends are friends forever if the Lord's the Lord of them…In the Father's hands we know that a lifetime's not too long to live as friends."* If I don't find a way to connect directly with these folks, at the very least I bring them to God in prayer.

Proverbs 17:17 "A friend loves at all times…"

FRIENDS 2

❋

*A*t the risk of sounding self-righteous, I work hard at rising above petty discords that seem to creep into almost every relationship. Easier said than done, I know. I may have "friends" who'll take issue with me on this, but I strive to live up to the old adage: "To have a friend, you need to be a friend." What kind of friend are you? Jesus challenges us to be willing to go so far as to lay down our own lives for a friend. There are days when I reflect on that challenge and think, "That's a bit too much, Jesus." At the highest level, He was foretelling the reason He would later die on the cross. At my level, as His follower, He's asking me to be alert to ways to serve my friends without expecting anything in return. To turn the other cheek and ignore imagined – sadly, even sometimes real – slights. And to continue to love them as He has loved me.

Romans 12:10 "Love one another with brotherly affection. Outdo one another in showing honor."

COUPONS

$\mathcal{N}$ow that we're into the "semi-retirement" scene, I've become more aware of clipping coupons, whether it's for groceries or an unlimited list of other household needs. I wasn't always this way. My friend Kathie managed to convince me to carry a small pouch within my larger purse, in which she encouraged me to accumulate a variety of coupons. As she said, "You never know where or when you're going to be shopping. If you always have them with you, you're ready for an unexpected stop and you can take advantage of the bargain that's staring you in the face." For the most part, her advice has had favorable outcomes. At a spiritual level, I understand the value of clipping coupons. One of our pastors used to describe Christ as the Great Couponer, who exchanged His life for our salvation. And I also appreciate the value of Scripture in terms of redeeming me in the face of Satan's unexpected onslaughts. Memorizing targeted Scripture verses is the equivalent of saving and then cashing in coupons.

Psalm 119:11 "I have hidden your word in my heart that I might not sin against you.".

RENEWAL

━━━━━━❋━━━━━━

I've told my friend Kate that not all of these devotionals are about her. We chuckled about that, but here I am – writing about her again. What's up with that? We first connected when we worked together in an elementary school. From there, we moved to her coffee shop that had been her forever dream. That didn't work out, and we eventually went our separate ways. A few years later, we reconnected in a women's Bible study God led me to put together. Those new beginnings were tentative at first. I realized she was protective of her own family and how some of the internal relationship issues were tearing at her heart. And she knew about my latest marriage stresses. God found a way to put us back together like 'Gorilla Glue.' We both celebrate the new and higher excitement level we experience when we've come back after falling away. It's better than ever, when God's in the center!

Proverbs 18:24 "A man of many companions may come to ruin, but there is a friend who sticks closer than a brother."

COFFEE SHOP

---❋---

J was waiting for a friend at a local coffee shop. I was a little early for our date, and my gaze wandered around the large, attractively decorated room. At one table there were three men of about the same age. At another I saw five women engaged in animated conversation. I realized this was a place where folks come not only for sweets and lattes but also for connection and communication. It was near a large office complex, and I concluded that co-workers also stop here for lunch and lively chatter. Friends getting together, office teammates huddling over a sandwich and coffee. The location provides a relaxed and intimate setting for people to connect with each other and share their hearts. You and I don't have to drive to a café to chat with God. Our favorite prayer chair in our living room works just as well. Sit right there, make a date with Him, and let the conversation begin.

Matthew 6:6 "But when you pray, go away by yourself, shut the door behind you, and pray to your Father in private. Then your Father, who sees everything, will reward you."

MY FRIEND MARY

I'm looking at that title, and thinking what a great honor it is for me to call her my friend. Mary and I have known each other for more than 30 years. We first met in the ladies' room in an office complex where we both worked for separate companies. I said something that made her laugh, and she asked what made me so full of joy. Our relationship took off from there. Over the years we've been there for each other during difficult times in our lives. We lived near each other until she married a wonderful man and moved to Arizona. The miles between us have made staying in touch a little less frequent. But when we do connect, given our history and the fact we're the same age, we have a warm platform for chatting about marriage, grandkids, our health, senior issues, politics – did I say our health? Not sure how Mary feels, but for me, whenever we talk, it's a little taste of heaven. Have a friend your own age? Treasure that as a gift from God.

John 15:13 "There is no greater love than to lay down one's life for one's friends."

CHURCH LADIES

---※---

*W*hen I was growing up, my parents and I and my brother would sit in the same section of the same pew each week at church. As an adult, without that parental "pressure," I figured I could sit anywhere I wanted. Well, guess what? Now in my early 70's, I take great pleasure in sitting right where I want, in a worship center seating 2,500-plus: the SAME SEAT every week! One great blessing in pursuing this habit is I get to sit behind three wonderful ladies who indulge the same habit. Julie and Shawna are single women with typical single-person issues; Carmen is married with a career in overseeing foster children and their living situations. In the moments prior to the service, we have fun learning about each other's previous week. Then we enjoy the gift of worshipping God together, regardless of our different life styles. And after the benediction, we wish each other God's blessings for the coming week. I think it's pretty cool!

Hebrews 10:24-25 "...not giving up meeting together, as some are in the habit of doing, but encouraging one another – and all the more as you see the Day approaching (v25)."

COME ON IN

❋

My friend Lynn's house was just two blocks away from the doctor's office where I had a brief, routine mid-morning appointment. So on the way home I stopped and knocked at the door. When she opened it, I could tell from her casual garb and absence of make-up she'd not been expecting any company. Yet she immediately broke into a smile and said enthusiastically, "Come on in!" What a warm, genuine welcome. What's more, it communicated immediate acceptance. I was glad I'd repressed an earlier "should-I-or-shouldn't-I" moment. As I reflect on that visit, I'm reminded that our Lord is similarly welcoming – instantly and unconditionally – when we approach Him in sincerity and humility. Jesus' death on the cross means we have direct access to Him, if we seek His forgiveness and cleansing. And the welcome mat is always out.

Revelation 3:20 "Here I am! I stand at the door and knock. If anyone hears my voice and opens the door, I will come in and eat with that person, and they with me."

DOUBLE DONNA

*J*Google'd my name, Donna, curious to learn its meaning. The Internet can be a dangerous resource. The first definition I found was in the Urban Dictionary, street-wise and sometimes vulgar. It defined Donna as "a very intelligent, smart, fun to be with, hot, and attractive girl who is very much taken and definitely not available." Golly! I can work with that. In Gaelic, it means "ruler of the world." That works for me too. More realistically, the name's origin in Italian is "lady." I recently reconnected with another Donna, a special lady with whom I had a brief but meaningful history. Several years ago she and her husband, along with my husband and I, were involved in local leadership roles in Celebrate Recovery. It was a time of intense spiritual healing for all of us. Seeing her now was like we'd never been apart. It could be because we share the name, as well as that personal history.

Ruth 1:16-18 "Where you go I will go and where you stay I will stay. Your people will be my people and your God my God (v16)."

SMALL GROUP

———————— ❋ ————————

*T*t's a privilege – not to mention an awesome blessing – to be part of a small group that meets every other week to focus on a Bible-based study. It's so refreshing to share God's word, in a secure, intimate setting, with female friends. One reason I call it a privilege is because I get to be the leader. We've learned that the more frequently we meet, the deeper the mutual trust grows, not only with each other, but with God and His promises. We can be comfortable talking about our troubles and concerns, and explore specific spiritual encouragements relating to our individual personal and family needs. One way to describe it is "doing life together." And as the group's leader, I get to spend more time in the Word preparing for our meetings. I'm continually amazed at the insights God provides me as I do this. If you're not in a Bible-based small group, it's time you got with it!

Matthew 18:20 "For where two or three are gathered in My name, there am I among them."

CURE FOR LONELINESS

——————— ❈ ———————

*W*hen I find myself slipping into loneliness, I lift my hands to Heaven and begin singing this reassuring hymn. Well, at least I start humming it.

"My God and I go in the field together; we walk and talk as good friends should and do. We clasp our hands, our voices ring with laughter. My God and I walk through the meadow's hue.

"He tells me of the years that went before me, when heavenly plans were made for me to be, when all was but a dream of dim reflection to come to life, earth's verdant glory see.

"My God and I will go for aye together. We'll walk and talk just as good friends do. This earth will pass, and with it common trifles. But God and I will go unendingly."

Colossians 3:15-17: "…as you sing psalms, hymns and spiritual songs with gratitude in your hearts toward God (v16b)."

SAVE YOUR FORK

We liked him a lot. No, we loved him. And his beautiful young family. Pastor Jeff, who later would officiate at our younger daughter's wedding, was serving his vicarage at the church we were attending. In layman's terms, that's like an internship leading to formal ordination. Preaching his first Good Friday sermon in our church, he began by describing what a great cook his mother was. He especially loved the fabulous desserts she created in her kitchen. Quite often, as she cleared the table of dirty plates prior to serving up dessert, she would caution the family, "Save your fork. The best is yet to come." Jeff went on to detail the despair and hopelessness the first disciples felt as they saw Jesus their Lord die on the cross. They lacked the hindsight we as Christians have today, knowing about Easter Sunday and the Resurrection. "Save your forks, folks," Jeff concluded, "the best is yet to come!"

1st Thessalonians 4:14-18 "After that, we who are still alive and are left will be caught up together with them in the clouds to meet the Lord in the air. And so we will be with the Lord forever (v.17)"

NEW WINESKIN

*T*he other day I read again about Jesus calling Levi (who was renamed Matthew) to become one of his 12 disciples (see Mark 2:13-17). A few verses later, Jesus uses a unique metaphor to describe the transformation of a person who confesses Christ as his Lord and Savior: "No one pours new wine into old wineskins. Otherwise, the wine will burst the skins, and both the wine and the wineskins will be ruined. No, they pour new wine into new wineskins (v22)." I thought of my good friend's husband who found himself tagged as an alcoholic, and who immersed himself in a 12-step recovery program. He recently received his 3-year chip signifying continuous "clean time," and was hosted at dinner by his sponsor, accountability partner, and small group. And he's now excited about stepping into a leadership role in the program. Praise God for his transformation! Yes, I get the irony of using Christ's wineskin metaphor here. But except for the alcohol content, it works.

James 4:10 "Humble yourselves before the Lord, and He will lift you up."

NICKNAMES

---❋---

*S*ome nicknames flow naturally from a person's profession or birth name. For example, a chef might be called Cookie. I still call our older daughter Missy (christened Michele), even though it's been over four decades since she was a toddler. The origin of other nicknames may be harder to trace. Our younger daughter Sarah Rebecca became – and sometimes still is – BooBot. It might have been her own attempt at her middle name when she was learning to talk. As for me, my mother-in-law called me Donder. She was a New England native, and that's how her strong regional accent twisted my name. And Don Lewis, father of the late movie actor Geoffrey Lewis (the Lewises were distant relatives of my in-laws), kept it simple whenever we were together: "Hi, Don." God knows us intimately. Scripture tells us He knew us even before we were born. But there are no nicknames with Him. As a believer, He honors me as His child, and my full name in its original form is written in the Book of Life – both now and forever.

Revelation 3:5 "The one who is victorious will, like them, be dressed in white. I will never blot out the name of that person from the book of life, but will acknowledge that name before my Father and his angels."

BIG LITTLE MAN

*T*o respect his privacy, we'll call him Pete. My husband and I had just accepted leadership roles in our local church's launch of Celebrate Recovery, a nationwide Christ-centered 12-step recovery program. Pete is an achondroplasia dwarf; my husband stands 6"5' tall. Pete was already in a more traditional recovery program for gamblers, an addiction he acquired to compensate for his appearance. After a couple of CR meetings, he approached my husband and asked if he'd agree to be Pete's accountability partner. Jerry quickly agreed, but was curious as to how he'd been Pete's choice. "Because you came up to greet me the first night," Pete said, "I knew you were the one." My husband persisted: "Why did you decide to worship here in our church?" Pete's reply: "On my first visit, the pastor preached on a verse from 1st Samuel. He said God looks on the heart, not someone's physical appearance. It's the first time I felt like I belonged somewhere."

1st Samuel 16:7 "The Lord does not look at the things people look at. People look at the outward appearance, but the Lord looks at the heart."

ALL-INCLUSIVE

———————— ❊ ————————

*M*y cousin Linda drove nearly seven hours to watch her 13-year-old granddaughter compete in Odyssey Of The Mind World Finals. It was happening on the Iowa State University campus not far from us, and we met for dinner. She's one of my favorite relatives, and this was a rare chance for us to be together. I wasn't disappointed. It was a fun evening of reminiscences. Her brother-in-law joined us; his wife Sue, Linda's sister, died of cancer a year ago. Linda's divorced, and I sensed the two of them were enjoying a wholesome companionship. At one point during our wide-ranging chit-chat, I asked him how he and his late wife Sue met. "Our high school lockers were next to each other," he said, "and I asked her to prom." It was a large rural school district. He lived on the north side of a metro area; Sue was in a small town four miles north. As he filled in the details, I'd forgotten he grew up in the Roman Catholic faith. "When I told my mom, she raised her eyebrows and warned, 'you know, son, there are *Baptists* up there!'" We had a big laugh. Later I thought about how God doesn't make those distinctions. As long as we confess Jesus as our Leader and Forgiver, He embraces all of us into the One True Faith.

1ˢᵗ Corinthians 12:13 "For we were all baptized by one Spirit so as to form one body – whether Jews or Gentiles, slave or free – and we were all given the one Spirit to drink."

NEEDY

$\mathscr{H}$e doesn't have any on the top of his head these days. But the growth of my husband's ear hairs is phenomenal! As a result, we schedule a few minutes once a week while he sits in a dining room chair and I use a battery-powered trimmer to cut back the seven-day forest. Our elder daughter stopped by the other day just as I was about to perform this weekly task. She seemed taken aback by my casual acceptance of his invitation to "do my ears, please." After we were finished, I reflected on how these seemingly mundane tasks shared within a 50-years-plus marriage can seem like selfish needs to the casual observer. The fact is, whether in the context of a marriage or any other committed relationship – including a congregation of the faithful — God invites us to share our legitimate needs with each other. It might not be to trim ear hairs, but He calls us into fellowship to share each other's burdens as believers in His grace and endless provision.

Mark 10:45 "For even the Son of Man did not come to be served, but to serve, and to give his life as a ransom for many."

WALKING FAITHFULLY

———————— ✳ ————————

"*I* just turned 80," she told me, "and I feel like I'm suddenly falling apart." She turned her head and gestured to one of her ears. "These are my new hearing aids," she said; they were so tiny I didn't notice them until she pointed them out. "And I need an injection in my knee soon." Rita and her late husband attended the same church with us several years ago, and I've encountered her many times since then when I've been in the shopping mall she frequents regularly. She and Tom were avid high school sports fans. She's followed my son-in-law's coaching career for years, and still attends athletic events year-round at the large high school near her home. This particular day I spotted her as she was finishing her daily mall-walking routine. Despite what she'd just told me, her looks belied her age. She wore tasteful makeup, her outfit was casual but up-to-date, and her perfume smelled wonderful. I admired her attitude and her vigor, and concluded her faithful walking regimen was a big part of looking and acting younger than her true age. Seeing her was a great reminder that God rewards us in so many ways when we walk faithfully with Him.

Genesis 17:1 "When Abram was 99 years old, the Lord appeared to him and said, 'I am God Almighty; walk before me and be blameless."

STEPPING OUT

❋

J believe there are times when we're already in possession of the gift, or gifts, with which God has
equipped us to accomplish a calling He's placed on our
heart. All we need is the motivation to step out and "get 'er
done." By contrast, we may have a burning desire to move
into a specific ministry, yet lack the gift or gifts to take us
there. As we seek through prayer to discern whether it's
a legitimate call on our time, God will supply us with the
talent. My good friend Mary has experienced this. She's at a
point in her life where she senses it's time to step out in new
or expanded relationships to share Jesus' love and forgiveness. One of her spiritual mentors counseled her this way:
"We're alive in His Spirit living within us, so He speaks
into our lives to give encouragement. The Lord is giving
you the 'gift of faith' to move you out into new territory.
There are times when God offers that gift in order for you
to believe in something you'd not considered before. Take
this gift and call out the gold in others to spur <u>them</u> into
new territory as well."

*Matthew 17:20 "Truly I tell you, if you have faith as small as a
mustard seed, you can say to this mountain, "Move from here
to there,' and it will move. Nothing will be impossible for you."*

REAL HEROES

---

*H*i. Jerry here. I'm Donna's husband. She's given me permission to pinch hit for her on this one. I was only 15 when the Chicago Cubs won their last World Series in 1908. Just kidding. But seriously, folks, it <u>has</u> been a long time. And this year it looks like the Curse of the Billy Goat, at long last, may be overturned. As I write this, the Cubs have the year's best won-loss record in all of major league baseball, on the strength of some All-Star Talent. I get goosebumps when I watch Jake Arietta pitch. And the hitting of Anthony Rizzo, Javier Baez, Ben Zobrist – true artists with the bat. But once the game ends, along with my victory-fueled euphoria, I remember these are simply human heroes, with human limitations – whose contributions were nothing more than part of a game! And then I remember the heroes of the Christian faith (Hebrews 11), and how their contributions were part of the greatest story ever told: God's plan for my redemption through the life, death and resurrection of Jesus Christ. Now, there's a <u>real</u> hero.

Hebrews 12:1 "Therefore, since we are surrounded by so great a cloud of witnesses, let us also lay aside every weight, and sin which clings so closely, and let us run with endurance the race that is set before us."

TEACHERS

*E*arly June brings with it the end of the school year, at least around here. Thinking about the gals in my Bible study who are employed in our local schools, and how they're "off the hook" for a couple of months, prompted me to reflect on my own grade school and high school years. I realize now that my teachers back then not only imparted knowledge about their assigned subject matter, they also instilled in me a respect for others – regardless of socio-economic status. And they reinforced the importance of moral behavior, manners, and just plain getting along with everyone around me. Yes, I know this sounds a lot like the gray-haired old timer: "In <u>my</u> day *blah blah blah…*" But I believe that's why I'm a peacemaker today. So here's a big THANK YOU not only to my parents but also to my long-ago teachers for what they did during my growing up years – and for who I am in Christ now.

Luke 6:40 "The student is not above the teacher, but everyone who is fully trained will be like their teacher."

CRAZY BUSY

————————— ❋ —————————

A friend and I were on the phone together, trying to find a day during the upcoming week when we could meet for lunch and just catch up with each other's lives. We weren't doing too well finding a common date, and she confessed, "I'm just crazy busy these days." At first blush, I understood what she was talking about. And then the part of me that's forever trying to analyze others' behaviors (my kids tease me about hanging out my shingle) wondered whether my friend actually meant her busy-ness was driving her crazy. No, really, I get it. I've been in that over-the-top busy mode myself, although it's been quite a few years. These days I'm concerned that more and more people around me – and probably around you, too – are complaining about being too busy to (fill in the blank). I'm concerned these scheduling overloads are blinding my friends and family to the <u>real and only </u>source of respite from "crazy-busy."

Matthew 11:28 Jesus said, 'Come to me, all you who are weary and burdened, and I will give you rest.'"

GOD'S PERFECT TIMING

————————— ❋ —————————

*N*ot even the most talented Hollywood screenwriter could craft a script more intriguing and heart-warming. My dear friend Mary shared with me that after nearly 20 years of estrangement from her three grand-daughters, as well as from their father (Mary's youngest son), there's been a blessed breakthrough. Brief backstory: Mary divorced her husband after 20 years of alcoholism and abuse, and moved several states away to start a new life. During the intervening years, she tried repeatedly to connect with her youngest son, but was constantly rebuffed. And during those years, Mary and I have been praying fervently that God would engineer a reconciliation. Recently, she sent still another text to the girls, all now in their 20's, asking if she could meet with them on their home turf. Not only did they say "yes", they asked how quickly the reunion could be arranged. Mary's elated. "They want me to come be with them!" she says. My friend has been walking by faith all these years, confident that God would answer this specific prayer in His perfect time. Guess what else? The girls' father, Mary's youngest son, has finally expressed a desire to reconnect.

Hebrews 11:6 "And without faith it is impossible to please God, because anyone who comes to Him must believe that He exists and that He rewards those who earnestly seek Him."

FEAR

FEAR

*E*ver find yourself feeling afraid, but you're just not able to put your finger on what it is that's causing you to be afraid? I've been there. Once in a while, I'm able to name the cause of my fear. But more often, I get frustrated trying unsuccessfully to figure out why I'm afraid – or even define what it is I'm afraid of. Sometimes I'm afraid of the unknowns hidden in my future. Sometimes it's the horrors seen in the daily TV news reports. Sometimes it's simply the fear of venturing outside my front door. These fears are real, even if the reasons giving rise to them are baseless. Here's a tip that works for me. Just speak the name Jesus out loud. Audibly claim His name as the source of your courage against myriad fears. Step out in the assurance that He will walk with you, and His shield will protect you from the fears that surround you. Psychiatry labels it "agoraphobia," a fear of unsafe or uncomfortable places or situations. I respect medical science, but I also know what the Scriptures promise.

Exodus 14:13 "Don't be afraid. Stand firm and you will see the deliverance the Lord will bring you."

UPSIDE-DOWN

❋

*I*f there were a documentary film retracing every single day of my earthy existence, there'd be enough drama, humor, sadness, excitement, blessings and heartbreak to fill an ocean. You'd think after seventy-plus years of navigating life's roller-coaster, I'd be prepared for just about anything. But I wasn't ready for the night my husband said he needed to go to the emergency room. When he told me what he was experiencing, I knew he was right. We made the trip, the healthcare professionals dealt with the issue, and now all's well again. What made the event especially troubling for me? He's always been the stoic, propping me up when my own health problems dragged me down. Now <u>he</u> was the patient. We wives often see ourselves as "steel magnolias," able to stare down the worst the day might bring. When the routine unexpectedly becomes UN-routine, and our world suddenly is upside down, Christ is all we have. He got me through that night in the ER – and He can get <u>you</u> through yours, too.

Isaiah 44:8 "Do not tremble and do not be afraid…is there any other Rock? I know of none."

INTIMIDATING SCRIPTURE

---------※---------

*A*fraid to dig into God's Word? A couple of ladies in one of my Bible study groups tell me they have difficulty setting aside time to read and reflect on Scripture. If you can relate, I suspect your reasons mirror theirs. It usually comes down to a daily work or household schedule that's so hectic there's no room for personal quiet time. Or so they say. During one such discussion, the real excuse slipped out. They confessed to being intimidated at the thought of spending time reading and meditating on the Scriptures. There's a fear the Word will convict them of their need for a deeper walk with Jesus. I offered that when such a feeling comes over you, that's a clear signal you're in need of the forgiveness and grace our Savior can provide. When you're most vulnerable, that's when you need God's correction and direction. You're experiencing a hunger and thirst that only the Bible's love story can satisfy.

2nd Timothy 3: 16-17 "All Scripture is…useful for teaching, rebuking, correcting and training in righteousness (v16)."

WIND CHILL

---※---

*A*t daybreak this morning, the temperature here was 7 below zero. Add in the wind chill factor and it was more like 27 below. As Iowa winters go, that's par for the course. Before brewing my first cup of coffee, I instinctively went for the thermostat and hiked it up a few more degrees from the overnight setting. I looked out my patio door, and saw two robins foraging for breakfast. Robins! I thought they went south for the winter…like any sane Iowan should do. I marveled that they'd not frozen in their tracks. My mind drifted to the laborers and construction workers whose jobs required them to be out in this weather. And then my heart focused on the homeless people in our metro area. How do they manage to survive in these conditions? I felt a little selfish as I snuggled into my prayer chair, lounging in the warm indoors. God, I prayed, please protect these animals. Much more than that, please protect these dear people.

Luke 12: 5-7 "Do not fear; you are more valuable [to God] than many sparrows (v7b)."

MEMORIES

*F*or this one to work, I need to tell you I've had two radical mastectomies, the first in 1984 and the second in 2007. Neither involved reconstruction. Fast forward to this recent Christmas. My daughter gave me a pair of jeans with some really neat bling-blings on the hip pockets. Wouldn't you know it? They didn't fit – so yesterday she and I headed off to exchange them for the right size. On the way, she said she wanted me to help her look for some new bras. I remarked off-handedly such a focused shopping trip would bring back memories. "No," she shot back, "you mean mammaries." We both laughed, and as I reflect back on those body-changing surgeries, I give God praise. First, because the long-term outcomes of both have been positive. Secondly, God's given me a sense of humor strong enough to shun self-pity and get on with life. I tell folks I can now mow the lawn without a shirt on. Third, my husband still loves me without my breasts.

2nd Corinthians 5:1 "For we know that if the earthly tent we live in is destroyed, we have a building from God, an eternal house in heaven, not built by human hands."

ROAD RULES

———————— ❋ ————————

*W*orking with my friend Kate in her coffee shop brought us in touch with Joe, a delivery man for one of our suppliers. Joe stopped once a week with our order, and – deeply spiritual man that he was – would engage us in conversation about Jesus and our relationship with Him. Kate kept a chalkboard on one wall of the shop for patrons' impromptu scribbles. On one visit, Joe wrote: "Jesus is the same yesterday, today, and forever." Joe had been driving semi's for years, and knew the rules of the road as dictated by his employer. They included warnings about swerving for animals in his path. One night, he instinctively jerked the wheel to avoid a deer; his truck fell off an overpass onto the street below, and he died in the fiery wreck. Our God is a loving and compassionate God, but throughout the Bible He lays down "rules of the road" for our physical as well as spiritual protection. He knows what harms can befall us if we revert to our human instincts and swerve off the path He's mapped out for us.

Deut. 6:1-19 "Fear God…by keeping all his decrees…so that you may enjoy long life (v2)"

ROBBED

————————✳————————

*A*n upscale coffee shop seems the unlikely scene of the theft of a wallet. But it happened – and it happened to me! My good friend and I met there for breakfast a few mornings ago. It was her birthday and it was my treat. I paid for our food and then dropped my wallet back into my unzipped purse hanging from the back of my chair. It wasn't until I got home a couple of hours later that I discovered the wallet was gone. I immediately returned to the coffee shop (no luck there) and also made sure I'd not lost or misplaced it myself. There wasn't a trace. And so I began checking off all the recommended action steps, including cancelling credit cards and notifying the driver's license bureau. When I spoke with a police detective, I learned two other customers had been "boosted" there that same morning. He offered words of sympathy, suggesting I might experience feelings of "violation," a common reaction of similar victims. You know what? I'm still a little fragile. But instead of feeling violated I find myself praying that I can forgive the thief, and that he or she will find Jesus.

Luke 11:14: "Forgive us our sins, as we forgive those who sin against us.

FEAR AND WISDOM

————————————❊————————————

*T*he recent theft of my wallet while I was enjoying a friend's company in a coffee shop gave rise to all kinds of fear. Would I suddenly be the victim of identity theft? Would my financial credit be compromised? Would an intruder try to break into my home? And then this phrase came to mind: "Fear is the beginning of wisdom." Was this an original thought? Or had I heard it somewhere before? Yes, I had! It was from Proverbs 9:10 "The fear of the Lord is the beginning of wisdom, and the knowledge of the Holy One is understanding." We experience fear during times of health issues, the loss of a loved one, betrayal by friends. It's only when we stop and look at reality through the eyes of faith that the storm clouds end and clear vision returns. God calls us to trust in Him and hand Him our fears in exchange for faith. Doing so leads to the wisdom that He will protect us.

Mark 4:35-41 "He said to His disciples, 'Why are you so afraid? Do you still have no faith?' (v40)"

NATIONAL MOURNING

*O*orry to say, but I'm growing weary of seeing the American flag flying at half-staff. Lately, it seems like this symbol of national mourning is happening every other day. I know that's an exaggeration, but the reality is, it's a visual I can do without. Why? Because it's an immediate, local reminder that somewhere in our country there's been a loss of life as a result of violent assaults on school campuses or involving the sacrificial deaths of first responders and law officers. As I write this, we're all still in shock over the deaths of five police officers and the wounding of several others in Dallas at the hands of a crazed sniper. According to USA TODAY, it's the 67th time President Obama has ordered flags at half-staff, "an act he has performed more than any other president in our country's history." Enough already! The apostle Peter urges us to "live in harmony with one another...do not repay evil with evil (1st Peter 3:8-9)." God promises to make tomorrow better if we'll humble ourselves before Him and obey His teachings.

Jeremiah 31:1-38 "I will turn their mourning into gladness; I will give them comfort and joy instead of sorrow (v13b)."

POLITICS

CAUCUS NIGHT

*W*e live in Iowa, where excitement comes in a variety of packages: corn, soybean and hog prices... the State Fair...and the presidential caucuses. Every four years we're the first in the nation to start the candidates' winnowing process. For 16 or more months prior to the national nominating conventions we're courted by every would-be candidate who draws breath. At the moment, this year's caucuses (comparable to other states' primaries) are less than four weeks away. It's getting to be a zoo. No exaggeration – we're getting robo-calls on our phone at the rate of 8 or 9 per day! We used to hunker down and do our best to ignore the circus. But this year, maybe not. Franklin Graham, Billy Graham's son, was in town the other day. He threw down the gauntlet: "We need Christians to vote for politicians that stand for Biblical principles and Biblical truth." My husband's decided to step up and attend a caucus for the very first time.

1 Peter 2:13-17 "Live as people who are free, not using your freedom as a cover-up for evil, but living as servants of God." (v16)

POLITICS

———————————✳———————————

*W*e're smack dab in the middle of a presidential campaign. Candidates of every political persuasion are vying for our support. I confess that most of them leave me cold. One or more of their positions on the issues that matter to me are contrary to my beliefs. On the surface, I'm feeling like each of them is pulling at me to ignore my conscience and vote for them because of a specific topic that trips my trigger. But down deep, I believe God is telling me to pray for <u>all</u> of them. He's telling me that every one of them has something positive to offer our nation in the way of leadership skills, but also that every one of them has a faith issue they need to address privately and personally. So I've been called to pray for them all, by name, that somehow God would raise one of them up to be the clear choice according to His full Word. And God's call on me is also to believe that He will fulfill His purpose through the right choice.

Daniel 2:21 "He changes times and seasons; he removes kings and sets up kings; he gives wisdom to the wise and knowledge to those who have understanding."

POLITICS 2

———————✻———————

*W*henever someone starts to talk politics with me, I bristle. One big reason is I've been there without having much choice, and not liking it! Long ago and far away, my husband "got involved." He ran successfully as our city's youngest city council candidate, and was re-elected to a second term. As a result, our state's powerful Republican Party saw him as a viable candidate for state legislature, and even beyond, as a congressional or gubernatorial hopeful. The preparation included me becoming the focus of the plan's "coach the wife" process. It wasn't pretty, I didn't like it one bit. While my husband was meeting with campaign strategists with connections to Gerald Ford and Ronald Reagan, I was being tutored on what to wear and how to act. Frankly, I hated it. Am I repeating myself? Looking back, it was a reluctant growing experience for both of us. He lost – I won. In terms of where we are now in our lives together, we understand the success of God's plan depends on our surrender to Him and His desires for us, not only as individuals but as His nation.

Daniel 6:28 "So Daniel prospered during the reign of Darius and the reign of Cyrus the Persian."

POLITICS 3

---***---

*T*he 2016 Iowa caucuses are history. In our state, the caucus is virtually the same as a primary election. The incoming recorded phone messages, the incessant TV commercials, and the endless posturing of a record number of presidential hopefuls, are finally over – at least until the respective parties' candidates are selected at national conventions this summer. Then, the final campaign drumbeats begin all over again. As I write this, it's been less than a week since our state's caucus results were published. Why should I be surprised at the results, even if it wasn't "my candidate"? After all, I've been praying fervently that God would raise up a leader worthy of our trust to lead our country for the next four or more years. While the caucus outcome wasn't what I personally would have preferred, why should I doubt that God has answered my prayers? I need to repeat that prayer until the November elections!

Ist John 5:14-15 "This is the confidence we have in approaching God: that if we ask anything according to His will, He hears us.(v14)"

PERSEVERANCE

FOOD FOR THOUGHT

---❋---

A recent day trip with my husband took us through southern Iowa's Amish country. I've had a long fascination with the Amish lifestyle and culture, although I've always been puzzled by what I've understood to be the works-dominated philosophy of their faith. But that's for another time. Our route took us through Bloomfield, where we stopped for lunch at CJ's Family Restaurant on the square across from the picturesque Davis County courthouse. CJ's isn't fancy, pretty much like any '50s and '60s corner luncheonette you'll find in a semi-rural small town. What caught my eye was a hand-painted sign board on the wall near us: "Live every minute with LOVE in your heart, GRACE in your step, and GRATITUDE in your soul." What a great recipe for daily living!

John 6:41-59 "I am the bread of life." (v. 48)

MARINATE

$\mathcal{M}$y husband and I enjoy cooking together; he's the one who likes to try new recipes. Some involve the use of marinades to penetrate and flavor certain cuts of meat. Marinades are often needed to tenderize the meat, too. For best results, overnight refrigeration is involved, allowing enough time for the marinade to soak in and achieve the desired flavor and tenderness. In his book <u>Tattoos On The Heart</u>, Father Greg Boyle introduced me to a new sense of the word "marinate." He presents several spiritual truths, punctuated with dramatic and sometimes tragic encounters with street gangs, and then challenges his readers to "marinate on this." If we regularly read God's Word, pray about what we read, and let it soak in throughout the day, we will be at peace. Circumstances may not always change, but joy will show up. Let the Scriptures be your spiritual marinade, tenderizing your heart and flavoring your actions.

Colossians 3:15-17 "Let the word of Christ dwell in you richly." (v.16)

GOD'S PLAN

———————— ✻ ————————

*K*ate finally realized her life's dream – to own a coffee shop unlike any other in town. She leased the perfect location, contracted with a famous industry consultant, bought the best espresso equipment, and hired me to help. Yet after a few years, the downside of retailing took its toll. Long hours were inevitable, and cherished family time evaporated. With a heavy heart, she sold the business. Neither of her next two jobs provided the fulfillment she sought. After a brief hiatus, she landed a position with Freedom For Youth serving disadvantaged teens and young adults. At first she thought she'd been hired in an administrative support role. But during a follow-up interview, she was told the organization was opening a coffee shop as an entrepreneurial learning opportunity for its young clients. "We want you to help train these kids," she was told. As she shared this with me recently, we agreed we serve an awesome God whose plans for us don't always coincide with our own. Even though Kate felt she'd involved Him in her own earlier business dreams, He had something bigger in store for her.

Jeremiah 29:11 "For I know the plans I have for you…plans to prosper you and not to harm you."

SCRAMBLED LETTERS

---❄---

*I*t was the Christmas season, and my husband's parents were visiting for the holiday. On this day – bright, still and crisp with freshly fallen snow – my father-in-law took our two young daughters for a walk through the neighborhood. An ageing drive-in movie theater was just blocks from our house. It still drew crowds during warmer weather, but the moveable letters on its ground-level marquee now declared "Closed For The Season." Running errands later that day, I drove past the site and glanced at the sign. It now read: "Closet For Noses." I turned to the girls in the backseat, and before I could say a word, both shouted in unison, "Grandpa did it!" Our lives are like the theater sign. Unexpected events, unwelcome slights from friends or family, sudden health issues, can scramble us and create uncertainty in our soul. By contrast, our God is unchangeable, immovable, always near and waiting to commune with us. He hears our groaning, and promises His peace if we will only seek it.

Hebrews 13:8 "Jesus Christ is the same yesterday and today and forever."

EXPECTATIONS

---※---

*F*or most of my life, I've been one whose expectations often go unfulfilled. I'm great at mental imagery – I picture in my mind how I want an event or personal interaction to turn out. And invariably, the actual outcomes disappoint me. They're usually way below the expectation I'd created in advance. It's happened with friends; worse yet, it's happened with family. Sadly, unless I choose to share these expectations, the friend or family member who's failed me has no idea what's going on. I have two options open to me: tell folks right up front about what I anticipate; or ask God for grace to accept the outcome, no matter what it looks like. The former can set the stage for family or friend's fear of failure and its related stress. The latter makes more sense to me. After all, Jesus makes it clear He expects me to live a life worthy of Him, but He also understands and forgives my "weak flesh." And He asks me to do the same with the person who's the focus of my unrealistic expectations.

Micah 6:8 "He has told you, O man, what is good; and what does the Lord require of you but to do justice, and to love kindness, and to walk humbly with your God?"

JUMP START

---❋---

*W*hat's your first-thing-in-the-morning routine? Shower? Coffee? Trot off to the Golden Arches for an Egg McMuffin? Check your Face Book page for overnight entries from your BFF? Here's a thought: talk to God before you talk to anyone else, before you do anything else. Okay, so maybe I have a cup of coffee alongside me. But my experience has been that saying "good morning" to God clears out the sleepy cobwebs and directs my thoughts to the positive priorities waiting for me on the day's do-list. It doesn't have to be a lengthy conversation. Save those chats for later in the day when you've set aside serious devotional time. Memorize Psalm 5:3 and say it out loud soon after you've awakened. Don't worry about disturbing your spouse. If that person is still sleeping next to you, tell yourself your sunrise sermonette will do wonders for him.

Psalm 5:3 "In the morning, oh Lord, you hear my voice...I lay my requests before you and wait in expectation."

TRUE JOY

———————— ❋ ————————

T know a woman who says she's been a Christian since childhood. We were in a couples Bible study years ago when she gave her testimony. To hear her tell it, she was born into a Christian home. That's all she ever knew, and she's never wavered from the faith since. Our paths still cross occasionally, including at church services. In each of those encounters, I've never once seen her smile. I don't get it. Although I too grew up in a "church family," it wasn't until a series of events in my adult life that I realized what it was to be not just a believer, but a committed follower of Jesus. I was struggling with my first bout of breast cancer, coping with a divorce, and trying to raise two teenaged daughters on my own. One morning I cried out, "God, I can't endure any more. Help me!" I can't begin to describe the sense of peace that washed over me at that moment of complete surrender. The issues didn't disappear, but for the first time in my life I felt able, with His strength, to cope. I now knew without doubt He held me in His hand. I call it JOY – and it makes me smile all day long.

John 16:24b "Ask and you will receive, and your joy will be complete".

DEEP WATER

*I*n these devotionals you'll find occasional references to stressful events in my life. My husband, now a fully-devoted follower of Jesus, says it's OK to tell you he's been the source of many of those blips on the radar. Truth to tell, a few of them were huge blobs. One of them led to a brief separation. I lived with our daughters during that time, and spent hours in God's Word, emptying my soul in front of His throne and praying for the road to reconciliation. After the fact, my sister-in-law told me she was "watching" from afar, amazed at my spiritual stamina and determination to push through. As we talked by long-distance phone, she thanked me for my example of being able to walk through those deep waters. Her word picture intrigued me, so we talked more. I understood that Christ was my SCUBA gear, allowing me to walk through those deep, deep waters, breathing His clean air and enabling me to reach the solid shore ahead of me. Read all of Exodus 14, and you'll get a sense of how God can accomplish miracles like this in your own life.

Isaiah 43:2 "When you pass through the waters, I will be with you; and when you pass through the rivers, they will not sweep over you."

THE MANGER & THE CROSS

---------------❋---------------

I'm a visual person. Right now, I'm imagining a picture of the Bethlehem manger, overlaid with the shadow of a Roman cross. Only God knows whether the infant Jesus in those early months of His earthly life understood that it would end at the cross. Scriptures tell us He was committed to His Father's plan from adolescence forward. And He lived such a blameless life that His death sentence seems a cruel injustice – at least in terms of our human understanding. Throughout his adult life, He was focused on the cross at the end of His road, never wavering, knowing it would result in not only victory over sin but also our being with Him for eternity. Can we be as bold and determined to keep our eyes fixed on the cross until the moment of our physical death? There are many potential distractions in this life. Keeping the Crucifixion – and His resurrection – in clear view, while we continue to celebrate the manger, gives us daily strength to overcome them and keep reaching for the cross.

1ˢᵗ Corinthians 1:18 "For the message of the cross is foolishness to those who are perishing, but to us who are being saved it is the power of God."

CARRY THE LOAD

————————— ✳ —————————

*I*t happened during one of our interstate household moves. We bought a split-foyer house in a nice neighborhood, but it needed some upgrading to meet our tastes and lifestyle. The kitchen was top priority. We reached out to a reputable local contractor to help us install new cabinets and an island separating the kitchen from the dining area. The day he came – alone — to hang the suspended cabinets, I realized how old he was. And I panicked when he lifted the entire unit by himself and staggered out to the front lawn where he collapsed, sucking air. The visual sticks with me to this day. I'm appalled at the number of times I've taken possession of ridiculously heavy spiritual burdens. God offers me the gift of bearing the load for me, but He needs me to intentionally surrender it to Him first. Never underestimate God's grace. Even if we're still carrying our portion of the load, His grace gives us the needed strength. Oswald Chambers says, "Don't just cast it aside, but put it over onto Him and place yourself there with it."

Psalm 68:19 "Praise be to the Lord, to God our Savior, who daily bears our burdens."

EXERCISE

———————✻———————

*E*xercise is NOT my thing. There've been distinct seasons in my life when I gave it my best shot. We bought a treadmill once. I set it up in our laundry room, and hung a small screen TV from the ceiling so I could watch it while I "treaded." I don't remember how long that lasted, but when we finally sold the machine, it was still under warranty. Then came the outdoor walking routine, and then the mall-walker routine. Neither of those regimens excited me, especially hiking through our neighborhood at 6 a.m. in sub-freezing temperatures. The mall walking lasted a little longer, but only because I'd stop and window shop, thinking those extra minutes of browsing could figure into the total exercise tally. God calls me to exercise my heart, brain and soul by being faithful in a daily routine of Bible reading, meditation and prayer. He wants me to be in top-notch condition to overcome the unexpected obstacles Satan puts in my path. God wants me to get to the finish line in one piece, so I can celebrate with Him in Heaven.

1st Corinthians 9:24-27 "Run in such a way as to get the prize.(v24b)"

EDUCATION

All but two of the women in the Bible study I'm currently leading are employed in the local public school systems. A couple of them are, or have been, elementary school teachers. The others have worked in administrative positions. They range in age from the early 30's to the early 50's. Regardless of their age differences, however, they're unanimous in lamenting government-imposed rules controlling official relationships between parent, child and teacher. In their view, time-tested techniques for maintaining classroom decorum and discipline have been trashed in favor of politically-correct and generally ineffective guidelines for teacher-student interaction. The result: challenging learning environments at best, especially in large classrooms, and near chaos at worst. And yet our teachers plod on. God bless them for their dedication and perseverance.

Proverbs 22:6 "Start children off on the way they should go, and even when they are old they will not turn from it."

BACKBONE

---------- ❋ ----------

*T*he layman's definition of osteoporosis is a weakening of a person's bone structure due to calcium loss, often linked to estrogen imbalance. My cumulative health issues over the years prompted my family doctor to prescribe a calcium supplement intended to slow or minimize the advance of osteoporosis. Not too long ago, he decided to end the prescription, and I opted to move forward on my own with an over-the-counter calcium tablet. Without an outpatient bone scan, I won't know how effective this will be. But I have faith that it's still beneficial to my overall wellbeing. On a spiritual level, I know that Satan seeks to rob me of my passion for following Jesus. His various tactics aimed at weakening me are described throughout Scripture. My daily devotional time, including time in the Word, and coupled with what I call "arrow prayers" throughout the day, give me the backbone I need to fend off Satan's attacks.

Ephesians 6:10 "…be strong in the Lord and in His mighty power."

DAYTONA 500

My husband's a big NASCAR fan. He's already checked the annual spring race at Talladega off his "wanna be there" bucket list. So it's no wonder he gets antsy when mid-February rolls around and the Daytona 500 marks the start of a new racing season. This year the checkered flag saw the closest finish in the track's history. After all these years I still don't understand a lot of what's going on. As we watched the telecast I did notice, though, that one of the two leading cars on the last lap (Matt Kenseth, if you're a junkie too) got bumped and wobbled off the pace, ending up 14th. I thought how sad, to have the finish line in sight and then lose the race. Our lives are often like that. Our own mistakes can be costly. But many times, through no fault of our own, we get bumped aside by the actions of others. God's there to lift us up, put us back on track, and energize us for a great finish.

1st Corinthians 9:24 "Do you not know that in a race all the runners run, but only one gets the prize? Run in such a way as to get the prize."

PERSEVERANCE

———————— ✳ ————————

The ice on our pond is slowly thawing. It'll be another two or three weeks before it's gone completely, unless the coming spring stalls out. But the local geese and mallards, hungry for open water after a long winter, were willing to settle for even the smallest ice-free pool. This morning I watched a mallard hen swim to the edge of the ice, and then climb out. It was fascinating. Instead of taking flight, which she could have easily done, she paddled furiously until her breast slid up over the lip of the ice – and kept paddling until her bulk was clear of the water. As I watched, the word "perseverance" came to mind. And I was reminded of the Apostle Paul's life struggles after he committed himself to the cause of Christ. As long as we keep our eyes focused on the Cross, God will provide us with what we need to push through any obstacle.

Philippians 4:11-13 "I can do everything through Him who gives me strength (v13)."

LENT

I grew up in a church whose traditions included giving something up for Lent. Mind you, it wasn't a "requirement." But as a kid, I was sensitive enough to peer pressure to realize I needed to forego a favorite food, treat or activity for the 40-day Lenten period – or have to answer friends' questions about why I didn't. As a married adult who's made several interstate moves over the years, including plugging in to a variety of church denominations during that time, I long ago "gave up" the "giving up." Now when I hear a friend speak of making a Lenten sacrifice, it's often something that sounds to me as superficial. Knowing that Christ made the ultimate sacrifice for me – giving His perfect, sinless life on the Cross as payment for <u>my</u> imperfect, sinful life – makes giving up popcorn, chocolate bars or peanut butter and jelly sandwiches seem almost sacrilegious.

Mark 8:35 "If you try to hang on to your life, you will lose it. But if you give up your life for My sake and for the sake of the Good News, you will save it."

AMBASSADOR

*E*very once in a while something I'm reading, in so many words, will insist that I'm an ambassador for Christ – and challenge me to act accordingly. For most of my adult life I've struggled with feelings of inferiority. So thinking of myself as an ambassador – defined simply as "the highest-ranking person who represents her own government while living in another country" – is pretty intimidating. Until I remember Jesus' 12 disciples. An unvarnished picture reveals them as "the dirty dozen," lowly everyday blue collar working people who did what they could with what they had to represent their Lord and Savior to the rest of the world. In that sense, I'm a blue ribbon ambassador. I want to be a voice for Jesus, sharing what He's done for me in the Bible studies I lead.

2nd Corinthians 5:20 "We are therefore Christ's ambassadors, as though God were making his appeal through us. We implore you on Christ's behalf: Be reconciled to God."

MARCH MADNESS

———————— ✳ ————————

I've always had a thing for the underdog. Maybe it's because from childhood through adolescence I rarely had any encouragement about my gifts or abilities. So when March Madness rolls around each year, I find myself cheering for the lower-seeded teams. These are the NCAA college teams that come from less visible conferences, or whose season performances allowed them to barely squeak into the post-season dance. So far in this year's first and second rounds, a record number of lower-seeded teams have moved on to the next level. In other words, these underdogs have figured out how to exploit the favorite teams' vulnerabilities to turn in a winning performance. As a result, the higher-seeded teams' smug reliance on regular season successes fails them in the clutch. God calls us to a winning life of humility and service to His kingdom on earth.

Matthew 23:12 "For those who exalt themselves will be humbled, and those who humble themselves will be exalted."

BIBLE HEROES

———————— ✻ ————————

*I*t took me several years of growing in my Christian faith before I began to really appreciate the Bible's heroes. Part of that appreciation was realizing how much my own life, and needs, paralleled the lives of those Biblical giants. And I don't mean in terms of physical size; rather, how much they depended on God to get them through the tough times and come out whole on the other side. Esther is one, Ruth is another. It could be I've embraced them because they're women. But there's a guy – Gideon – who's right up there too. Gideon had it all figured out, how he was going to recruit a mighty army to defeat the enemy. But God challenged him to send the majority of the soldiers home, and to trust God to produce a victory with a hugely understaffed militia. It's a great, and sometimes gory, tale (see Judges Chapter 7). My take on this story is I need to rethink my own strategies for dealing with life's issues and consult God first before taking action.

Judges 6:11-24 "The Lord turned to him and said, 'Go in the strength you have and save Israel out of Midian's hand. Am I not sending you?' "

PUBLIC SERVANTS

*Y*ears ago I remember seeing a public service TV spot praising police officers. "You wouldn't go down that darkened alley for a million dollars," the ad copy read. "A cop does it for a whole lot less." Today, our metro area is reeling in the wake of the deaths of two Des Moines police officers. They died tragically, together, in the line of duty, and according to official records, they were the 27th and 28th Des Moines cops to give their lives in public service. My husband's a retired volunteer firefighter. He and his department felt personally bereaved in the wake of 9/11, so I appreciate from his perspective the impact these kinds of LOD deaths can have on a community. The funeral for one of the Des Moines officers was held at our church. In his eulogy, the police chief admonished the hundreds of uniforms in the auditorium: "Never forget why you signed on."

1st Peter 3:15 "But in your hearts revere Christ as Lord. Always be prepared to give an answer to everyone who asks you to give the reason for the hope that you have."

WORLDLY TROUBLES

---✳---

*T*he older I get, the more I seem to zero in on the smallest of life's irritants, whether it's within my own circle of influence, or in the world at large. You'd think at my age I'd have mastered the art of letting the little things go and focusing on the issues that really matter. Easy for you to say. For better or worse, it's my nature to take everything to heart, no matter its magnitude or insignificance. To me, it's ALL important. I'm a fixer. I want to make all things right, whether it's in my neighborhood or across the globe. Even if there's not the slightest chance of that happening. In my quiet time, God comes to me through His Holy Spirit, pats me on the head, and says, "Let it go, Donna. I'm the One who's in control here. Give it up."

John 16:28-33 "I have told you these things so that in Me you may have peace. In this world you will have trouble. But take heart! I have overcome the world (v.33)."

WASHING WINDOWS

———————❋———————

*E*veryone who knows me understands I'm a neat freak. Some of my close friends have asked me to help them clean their houses because they know how obsessive I am about tidiness. Two or three of them have even offered to pay me to clean. What a hoot! Seriously, during the winter I'm able to fuel that compulsion by indoors housekeeping. But I have to work hard to ignore the grit and grime coating the outside of my windows. Now that spring's arrival is for real, I've finally scrubbed the other side of the glass. The spiritual imagery isn't lost on me. I realize the window to my soul can become clouded by greed, anger, lust, selfishness – the list goes on. Kneeling before God, confessing all the dirt, asking His forgiveness and accepting His grace, is like magical Windex. Not only can God now see into my heart and view the person He created me to be, I can clearly see Christ standing beside me and drawing me closer to Him.

1ˢᵗ Corinthians 13:12 "For now we see only a reflection as in a mirror; then we shall see face to face. Now I know in part; then I shall know fully, even as I am fully known."

PRAYER BLESSINGS

❋

*T*his whole business of God-centered prayer is a package of you-me-everybody blessings that will forever defy my limited ability to explain. In humility, I confess I'm known within my circle of family and friends as a faithful prayer warrior. But when I pray, you know what? I get more than I give! Especially when I'm praying for someone or something that's been brought to me through a third-party request. There's no doubt in my mind God will answer prayer, even though He sometimes has an answer beyond what we're expecting – and, in the long run, an answer that provides a far greater blessing than we sought. That's one of the awesome dimensions of our prayer relationship with Him. Simply put, I know that God will provide what He has in mind for the person or situation for whom I'm praying. But along the way, He's going to bless me with not only the confidence of His reply but also with the knowledge He's sustaining me in my own unspoken needs.

Romans 8:26-27 "We do not know what we ought to pray for, but the Spirit himself intercedes for us through wordless groans...(v.26)"

MARATHON

------------✳------------

T've come to realize prayer isn't a sprint, it's a marathon. Several months ago I saw the film "War Room". It inspired me to create a prayer cubicle in our home, with a pin-up board detailing specific on-going prayer requests for family, friends and our nation. Just last week my Bible study group and I watched the movie again. Together we acknowledged not only the power of prayer but also God's call for each of us to be relentless in our prayer life. In its most basic form, prayer is an intimate, honest and passionate one-to-one conversation with God. Beyond that, I believe He wants me to engage with Him on a daily basis to lay my fears, desires and concerns for others before His throne in a candid plea for His provision and intervention. I've seen ample evidence of answered prayer over the years, and so I press on in faith and a conviction that whether today, or tomorrow, or someday, I will hear from Him with the answers He knows will be the perfect reply. As Sir Winston Churchill said, "Never give in, never give in, never, never, never…"

Luke 18:1-7 "Then Jesus told his disciples a parable to show them that they should always pray and not give up…(v.1)"

LAXADENTICAL

———— ❋ ————

*M*erriam-Webster isn't likely to take note. But I've coined a new word: *laxadentical*. It's an adjective describing my husband who's been lackadaisical about scheduling his next dental appointment. Despite years of marvelous all-around health, for which we both praise God, he recently learned two crowns are needed to protect chipped teeth. Even though we have good insurance coverage, the out-of-pocket tab could be sizeable. Add to that what probably should be his first-ever visit to a podiatrist. The hours he spends on his feet each week at his part-time kitchen job at a supermarket are starting to take their toll on his feet. He's dragging his feet – no pun intended – on that one, too. His head is in his pocketbook right now, and I appreciate his financial responsibility. The bigger picture, though, is protecting his good health. Scripture tells us the same holds true with sin in our lives. The longer we ignore it, the more it overwhelms us and creates a chasm between us and God. He tells us that if we confess it's there, He'll remove it and allow us to move on in life with Him.

Isaiah 1:18 "Come now, let us settle the matter," says the Lord. "Though your sins are like scarlet, they shall be as white as snow; though they are red as crimson, they shall be like wool."

OUR POTENTIAL

————————— ✳ —————————

*D*o you ever wonder whether you're living up to your potential? Especially your God potential? I'm not sure I'm ready to draw a distinction between what the world says we're capable of, and what God calls us to do. I do know God created us to (a) worship Him, and (b) bring others into His family through our personal witness. The specific vehicle for that personal witness is the variable here. I spent some time today thinking about that. Here I am, at age 72, writing devotionals. What's up with that? Then I wondered whether I'd wasted time and talent in earlier years by ignoring His calling, or at least missing some hints as to what He wanted me to do for Him. Until now, I never had the slightest interest in writing. I do know I can call on Him to reveal the gifts He's blessed me with, and wait for Him to show me how He wants me to use those gifts. As Professor Paul Yost of Seattle Pacific University wrote about human potential, "(Christians) can risk doing the right thing because they are confident God is in tomorrow's unknown."

1st Corinthians 7:7 "...each of you has your own gift from God; one has this gift, another has that."

RESCUE

*H*ave you ever felt trapped in a situation you feel is hopeless? That you can't escape, no matter how hard you try on your own? Or even that you simply can't see it ending, that it's destined to go on forever? I have – and at more times in my life than I'd care to detail. There's been betrayal by friends, more times than I can count. There's been cancer, twice. There's been divorce, once (praise God, my first husband and I remarried – although we have fun introducing each other to new friends as "my current spouse."). Take it from me, there is an unfailing lifeline: the cross of Jesus. OK, you're saying, how can it be that simple? Well, it does take faith that God will lift any of these burdens from you if you ask Him. But what do you have to lose? Follow my example. Just imagine He's sitting on the couch next to you. Tell Him how you're feeling, what you're struggling with, how you're ticked off at (fill in the blank). Empty your heart, and experience how He will fill it with His peace – to forgive, to persevere, to carry on.

Psalm 40:1-3 "I waited patiently for the Lord; He turned to me and heard my cry (v1)."

HAPPY FEET

❋

$\mathcal{F}$or several months my husband wore work shoes one size too small. He'd bought them on sale, trusting the initial in-the-store "just right" feel. He works part-time at a local supermarket, standing and walking 7 or more hours at a stretch. He finally admitted the corn pads and moleskin patches he used to mask the discomfort were no longer working – and promptly ordered a new pair of shoes the right size. At the end of his first workday wearing the new ones, he observed, with a big smile, "When the feet are happy, the whole body's happy!" You know me. When I heard him say that, my mind jumped instantly to the Apostle Paul's first letter to the Corinthians. He reminded them that they – as the body of Christ – needed to view each believer as part of the whole. Modeling ourselves after Christ, we must reach out to those who are hurting and serve them according to their needs and our abilities. My daily prayer is that God will put someone in my life that needs to hear His Word, and feel my loving touch.

1ˢᵗ Corinthians 12:25-26 "…there should be no division in the body, but that its parts should have equal concern for each other. If one part suffers, every part suffers with it; if one part is honored, every part rejoices with it."

STAYING YOUNG

❋

*N*ot long ago, I attended the funeral of a 90-year-old man. At the church luncheon after the service, we stood in line with people clearly in their 80's and early 90's. We were the out-of-towners; they were the locals who'd known the deceased for decades. I eavesdropped on their conversations as we moved closer to the green bean casserole, homemade potato salad and ham sandwiches: "What do you think about the latest prescription drug prices with your Medicare Part D? Have you seen Fred lately? Did his kids finally put him in that Alzheimer's unit over in Center Point? When's the last time you went to the Wednesday noon potluck at the senior center?" I'd been fussing for a few weeks before that funeral about how best to manage my own ageing process with grace and dignity. I decided that day, in the funeral lunch line, that one of the best ways is to honor the friendships I've developed with the 30- and 40- and 50-year-old women who've migrated into my circle. These ladies – mostly the ones in my Bible study groups – are the tonic that will keep me thinking young. They remind me that I'm only as old as I think I am.

2nd Corinthians 4:16 "Therefore we do not lose heart. Though outwardly we are wasting away, yet inwardly we are being renewed day by day."

GROWING OLD

--------------- ❋ ---------------

*D*espite what you may think, after you've read several of these devotions, I am <u>not</u> obsessed about growing old. I'll admit that I ponder the process and observe the obvious: the wrinkles, the wrinkles on wrinkles, the sagging skin, the hair loss, the flabby arm "wattles". And that's just my husband! I don't need a mirror to be acutely aware it's happening to me, too. We're in our early 70's, married for more than half a century, and until just recently paid little or no attention to this phenomenon called "growing old." Praise God for our continued good health, with only a brief hiccup or two along the way. I pray He'll keep on blessing us not only with good physical and spiritual health but also with healthy relationships – with each other, with family, and with loving and supportive friends. More than that, though, my daily prayer is He'll give me the peace to embrace whatever stage in life I'm in, with neither regrets about the past nor worries about the future. The best news of all is that I know how my story will end – with Jesus in Heaven forever.

Hebrews 11:1 "Now faith is confidence in what we hope for and assurance about what we do not see."

CONCLUSION

━━━━━━━━━❊━━━━━━━━━

*E*ven though I don't know you personally, this book of devotional thoughts may be my only chance to get in your face before you're standing at the threshold of Eternity. Because of what God has done for me, I'm passionate about following the Apostle Paul's example: "I try to find common ground with everyone, doing everything I can to save some. I do everything to spread the Good News and share in its blessings." (1st Corinthians 9:22(b)-23 NLT)

Do you truly trust Jesus as your Savior, knowing that your sins are forgiven? And do you know that He stands beside you as your defense attorney, in front of a Holy God, on that day you'll be called to account for your earthly life? If you don't know that you know that you know, please take time to find someone close to you who's committed her life to Jesus Christ – and be brave enough to ask her to share her own story with you. And if you're not comfortable doing that, please email me and let's arrange a one-on-one, heart to heart chat to talk about the condition of *your* "receiver" (see photo next page).

No matter where the future takes you, I promise you I will be your faithful Prayer Warrior. How can I do that when I've not even met you? Well, you're reading this now, so you're someone God knows and so I can pray for you as a member of His universal family. Here's how the Bible puts it in Colossians 4:12: "[Donna] who is one of you and a servant of Jesus Christ…is always wrestling in prayer for you, that you may stand firm in all the will of God, mature and fully assured."

ABOUT THE AUTHOR

*H*er father was a Special Agent with the FBI when Donna Mae (Ochs) VanHorn was born in the shadow of the US Capitol. While she was still a baby, the family moved to Milton, WI, where both of her parents' families had roots. It was home to Milton College, founded in 1844 as a religious academy by the town's settler Joseph Goodrich. No, she wasn't the first graduate, but she did meet her future husband Jared while both were students there in the 1960's. After graduation, they relocated to RI, Jerry's home state, where he accepted an editorial position with The Providence Journal. Later job and household moves took them back to her home state, and eventually Iowa. Donna's professional career has spanned several administrative support positions with such diverse employers as Iowa Bar Association, Xerox, National Pork Council, and West Des Moines, IA, municipal government.

Describing her observation skills, Donna says: "People wonder how, or whether, God speaks to them in this age. Without question, the Bible is God's campaign speech to His followers. That's my baseline. From there, when I see something – or something steps on my toes – I ask God, 'Anything here You want me to learn? What are You saying to me today?' " She remembers traveling with her mother who would be gazing out the car window and then suddenly blurting out, "I wonder what that telephone pole is thinking." Donna says, "I know she wasn't crazy. She was just in tune with the moment."

Today, she and her husband live in retirement in a Des Moines, IA, suburb. They serve their two adult daughters and their families in a variety of ways, and worship at Lutheran Church of Hope, one of the ELCA's largest congregations. Donna is a mentor to younger women, and leads a women's Bible study in her home. This devotional series is her second publication. She can be reached at dvstrawb43@gmail.com.

CPSIA information can be obtained
at www.ICGtesting.com
Printed in the USA
FSOW03n0638251116
27797FS